THE ULTIMATE
PARENTING MAP TO

MONEY SMART KIDS

THE ULTIMATE PARENTING MAP TO
MONEY SMART KIDS

LINDA LEITZ

A BRIGHT LEITZ MONEY MAP BOOK
bright leitz publishing

DEDICATION

This book is dedicated to Dallas, Erica, and Lizzie, who have taught me to appreciate the glory of individuality, and to Butch—my husband, the father of my children, and the man of my dreams.

ACKNOWLEDGEMENTS

Many people helped me on this project. I'd like to thank a few of them here.

Many people have shared their parenting ideas as well as their good and bad experiences in learning about money. I appreciate the candor of all of them and respect their privacy.

Thank you to Lynne Miller, Pam McKenzie, Denise Cuthbertson, Phil Watson, Rebecca Preston, Lisa Ellis, and Loretta Simonson for being test readers and proofreaders. Nancy Bernard also did these jobs and was a huge help with research and brainstorming ideas.

I'm grateful to David Drucker, Jettie Kootman, JJ Smith-Moore, Rebecca Mead, and Edie Spain for sharing their experience in writing and publishing. Also, Karen Leitz was wonderful to help with the editing process as we got into proofreading.

A special thanks goes to Rhonda Winchell who consulted with me heavily on the publishing and marketing details for this process. I appreciate her balance of realism and vision.

My business partner, Jane Young, has been supportive of many of my efforts that simultaneously augment what we do at our financial planning firm and take my time from it. Paulette Weaver and Terri Schlabs with our firm have also been great cheerleaders.

And of course, my family has been more wonderful than words can express.

INTRODUCTION

This book can be a great road map in helping your kids learn to use money and have a healthy relationship with it. Ideally you can read this cover to cover and it will get you off to a good start. Part I gives an overview of the process and philosophy of this successful teaching method. Part II gives some specific "how to" ideas on individual financial topics. Besides getting you started, Part II can be a good reference you can go back to as the issues surface.

While parenting is an ongoing learning process, don't assume that if something doesn't work immediately, you're doing it wrong. If you fall off the horse, get back on. As you keep at it, you'll find some very satisfying results and you'll find some solutions that work particularly well for you—some of which you'll develop yourself as you gain confidence.

Teaching your kids financial responsibility is an important job, but it can be fun. So enjoy yourself.

"I long to put the experience of fifty years at once into your young lives, to give you at once the key of that treasure chamber every gem of which has cost me tears and struggles and prayer, but you must work for these inward treasures yourself. "

– Harriet Beecher Stowe

bright leitz publishing

Copyright © 2006 Linda Leitz. All Rights Reserved.

Printed in the Canada. No part of this publication may be reproduced, stored in a retrieval system or transmitted in any form or by any means electronic, mechanical, photocopying, recording or otherwise without the written permission of the publisher.

ISBN 0-9773683-090000
Printed in Canada

THE ULTIMATE PARENTING MAP TO MONEY SMART KIDS

TABLE OF CONTENTS

PART ONE

Money. Who needs it?.....21
Financial illiteracy in general and in youth
Positive effects of understanding money

How to teach.....29
Projecting attitudes about work, money, and the cost of living
Talking to kids about money
Values and money

Where money comes from....39
Earning a living
Investments

Choices, relative values, and trade-offs.....45
What does a candy bar cost?
How much work or allowance it costs to buy what you want
You can't have it all—needs versus wants

Setting parameters....53
Establish what is not an acceptable use of money

Bailing kids out

The cost of mistakes—now versus later

Using money for enforcement.....59
Logical consequences

Beware of overemphasizing money

Getting started.....63
Respect individuality

Can't save people from themselves—at any age

PART TWO

Allowance..69

Bargains..77

Budgeting..81

Careers...85

Checking Accounts............................89

Credit Cards.....................................93

Debt Used Wisely..............................97

Discretion.......................................103

Divorce, Money, and Kids................107

Earning Money................................109

Education Funding..........................115

Future Goals..................................117
Gifts...121
Grandparents...................................125
Investments.....................................127
Jobs...131
Living Expenses..............................135
Pets...139
Philanthropy...................................143
Rewards..147
Savings..151
Siblings..155
Taxes...159
Vacations..163
Vehicles...167
Final Note.......................................171

THE APPENDIX

Future Goals...................................175
The Beauty of Investing..................176
Living Expenses..............................179

PART ONE

Money, Who Needs It?

"Parents owe their children a set of decent standards and solid moral values around which to build a life."
--Ann Landers

Every time you and your grade schooler go shopping, it turns into a battle of wills. She asks for every toy and snack that you pass. You want to let her have a treat, but each time you buy her something, she wants something else.

Your junior high student refuses to wear anything but designer jeans. Every school outfit you buy is passé within a month. The cost of clothing and weekends hanging out at the mall are out of control.

When you refuse to buy your teenage son a muscle car, he gets a job at a fast-food restaurant working evenings and weekends. Soon he has bought the car, but as time goes on, his grades decline as does his attitude. Then the transmission on the car goes out. He can't use the car to get to his job any more, but the monthly bills for his car insurance keep coming.

Kids and money. Sometimes the financial demands from your children make you feel like money flows through your fingers like water. Educating your family about money management can help you and them. At a surprisingly early age, your children can begin understanding basic monetary concepts and begin making financial decisions. Developing a system to teach your children responsibility regarding finances can allow you to gain greater control over spending without spawning arguments. It can also help your children to grow into financially responsible adults. During this process, you can find that fewer of their daily financial decisions need to be made by you. Your job can evolve much more into that of a policymaker and facilitator.

Most young people who graduate from high school know nothing about budgeting and can't even balance a checkbook. An alarming number of recent college graduates find that their first major adult challenge is digging out of debt. They have added frivolous credit card balances on top of their student loans, and the ability to keep their heads above water financially is limited at best. You may even feel that you are crippled by financial illiteracy. It's not too late to take control of your finances and to give your children the chance to avoid negative financial situations. You can give them the tools to be in control of their finances, and thus, be on the way to being in control of their own lives.

Comfort with money and the role it plays in life can make a huge difference in someone's outlook. As the understanding of basic financial concepts starts to take hold, children can begin to get a sense of their own financial priorities. That doesn't mean, of course, that they won't experience a learning curve. But it's so much better to learn at a young age—when food, shelter, and clothing are already a given—than to have to go through bankruptcy as an adult or to realize in their sixties that they won't ever be able to retire.

The first building block of learning financial responsibility is the concept that each financial choice has consequences. A child is capable at an amazingly young age of learning that if she spends money on something now, she won't have that money to spend on something else later. She can also learn to save money over time for something she wants. Access to some money of her own at an appropriate age will give her the joy of deciding what is important to her financially. She'll have the satisfaction of making her own purchasing decisions. This is the beginning of being a savvy consumer.

There are several benefits for you in this whole process. One benefit is that, as your children get older, fewer of the decisions about what to buy your children will fall to you. You can set parameters for what acceptable purchases are, then give the children choices within those guidelines. After you have given allowance or earning opportunities to your children, they will either have the money to buy what they want or they won't. Setting the guidelines of what your kids may buy and giving praise—or sympathy—for decisions made will be the lion's share of your job relative to the children's monetary decisions. The focus will shift from you being the money gatekeeper—because you didn't let them have something—to the consequences of the decisions the children have made themselves.

In many relationships, there either seems to be too much or too little information available about money. Many people are too eager to share how much an expensive trinket costs. They won't talk, though, about how much they make if money is tight or how much they have in credit card debt. Even within some families, one spouse doesn't know what is involved in family finances. While it would be difficult for any one individual to change this in our society, you can make a difference in how much your family knows about money and the role it plays in your life. That doesn't mean that you need to make money the center of your universe. It's an important part of your life and putting it in perspective can give your children a much healthier attitude toward finances than refusing to talk about it or only telling what they want to hear. It's like anything that's important to talk about with your kids—drugs, sex, emotions. If you aren't willing to discuss it, they'll get information from somewhere else. It can lead to false assumptions, obsessions, and even addictions.

Many people are fond of saying that "money is the root of all evil." This is actually misquoting a Bible verse from I Timothy which says, "The love of money is the root of all evil." So it's not money, it's loving it, that can be a problem. That concept goes the other way, too. Hating money or fearing it can be emotionally damaging. As with anything, putting too much emphasis on money—good or bad—can foster an unhealthy financial attitude that can last a lifetime.

Money is a tool. Just as you wouldn't turn your child loose with a chainsaw without giving him a few pointers on that tool's safe operation, you shouldn't just assume that your child will learn about money when he gets his first job. That will definitely be a great learning experience for him, but he can learn lots before he gets a first paycheck or even has to go to an interview. One of my children asked the other day how we learned how to do everything. I knew that nobody knows how to do "everything" and in digging into what she meant, she gave same examples. "How do you know how to put gas into the car? How did you learn what to do at the grocery checkout?" The answer is a combination of

(1) seeing what others do,

(2) asking some questions, and

(3) giving it a try.

That's also the best way to learn about money.

So what can you do to set up that type of financial learning environment for your children? First of all, give serious thought to what you can include them in and show them about how you and the family as a whole receive and use money. Second, encourage your kids to ask questions about money and ask them questions that make them take finances into their decision making process. Third, give them opportunities to make financial decisions and experience the outcomes of their own decisions. We'll look at the teaching method in more detail later.

When your kids have a good understanding of how money affects them, it's a relief to you in ways you might not have anticipated. The foundation of this method of teaching kids about money is that you make information available to them, set up the ability for them to make choices about how they use money, and allow them to learn from experience how their choices affect them. In the case of your child's first exposure to money, you begin to let her know that it's not up to you to get her every toy she wants. She'll have a budget or her own money and she decides—within limits—what she gets and what she doesn't. As she gets into middle school or junior high, she'll be able to take a greater role in deciding what discretionary purchases she makes. By high school, she can begin to make her own clothing purchases and be involved in whether or not she has a car. This helps to avoid battles with your children about whether they get the designer jeans or the generic brand, two dolls or one, the muscle car or a safe, modest sedan. Most importantly, it establishes early in your child's life the idea that she will ultimately be financially responsible for herself.

Many parents make every decision for their children until the kids get their first jobs. Then the parents wonder why their young adult offspring make such thoughtless financial choices. Let's face it. We're all going to make a few careless choices. Would you rather "repossess" a stereo from your twelve-year-old child because he borrowed part of the money from you to buy it or have him in bankruptcy in his twenties because he never learned how to use debt wisely? The early "repo" lesson makes a big impact on his attitude about debt and it's much less expensive over his life than the later bankruptcy lesson.

Of course, it's not all a bed of roses for you. Most of us would rather endure pain than see our child endure it. It's important, though, that you let lessons be learned by your child firsthand. If you always step in, you're teaching him that you'll always save him from his mistakes. And he'll expect that you'll do so for the rest of his life. Besides having to watch some difficult experiences, there's another equally difficult lesson for you to learn. Your children won't always make the same decisions as you. After all, you're not rearing your children to be clones of you. You're giving them the opportunity to become themselves. So you need to give them the latitude to make decisions that make them happy, even if the decision is not a choice you'd make.

Releasing control frees you and allows them to feel responsible for themselves as early as possible. It frees you from feeling that you need to make every little decision for them. It gives them a sense of control over their own decisions, which has a good chance of increasing their appreciation of you when they're adults. It frees you up to devote attention and money to saving for your own financial independence. One of the fears that many parents share is that they'll be a financial burden to their children some day. If you entertain every whim of your kids and don't put money toward your own future, that nightmare of geriatric dependence has a greater chance of coming true. If they realize that you aren't a living safety net for them, they'll be motivated to take charge of their own finances in their teens and twenties.

When your kids are young, allowing them choices is freeing to you because you make clear that it isn't your job to decide which trinkets and fads they throw money at. You may actually be funding their purchases, but the money comes to them in a way they understand and can largely predict. Also, they decide what to spend it on. "Can I have it?" can be answered with "I don't know. Do you have that much money?" Perhaps you can lead into a conversation about what she was planning on buying with what she has saved. Maybe it's a shirt, the latest music, or an outing with friends. Then you can discuss which item she'd rather have, if she can wait to have one of them, or if there's another alternative to getting either one.

Give your children the proper outlook about how to address the difference between their needs and their wants. To paraphrase those great financial mavens, the Rolling Stones, you can't always get what you want, but if you try, you'll get what you need. Furthermore, the right outlook will make you very satisfied with having what you need.

Personal Notes

How to Teach

"Train up a child in the way he should go: and when he is old, he will not depart from it.
-Proverbs

There are three basic techniques to use in teaching your children about money: hands on experience, example, and conversations. For most kids, these techniques are listed in the order of their effectiveness. When combined properly, they can work toward your child having a thoughtful process of how he deals with money. The hands-on experience—learning by doing—is key to effective learning. Teaching by example and discussion will bolster the learning experience to the extent that both are done effectively and the child is interested, but the child's direct experience is the key.

The foundation of the philosophy of teaching through experience is to let him have an increasing amount of control as his knowledge grows. In the child's initial exposure to money, give him a few acceptable alternatives from which he can choose for his financial decisions.

Part II of this book gives some particular strategies to use for specific financial areas. Set up choices that are within your family's moral constraints. As he gets older, he might not need to be given alternatives and he can choose without your input. Even when specific alternatives aren't used, be willing to answer questions about what is and isn't acceptable use of money and impose consequences for morally unacceptable decisions. But—and this is key—allow your child to make choices that are different from the decisions you would make. As with all good parenting, teaching your child about money doesn't mean that you are creating a replica of yourself. It's allowing the child to create his own financial identity. Within any range of acceptable choices, your child may land on the one that's the opposite end of that spectrum from you, but he's very happy with the outcome. Be prepared to allow that. He might decide that money is more important to him than it is to you or that he'd rather have a simpler life than the one he had growing up. Let that unfold to him.

Your child will also make some mistakes during his hands-on learning. Resist the temptation to save him from his errors. Making some mistakes and dealing with the consequences is much easier when he's young than when he's grown. Think about it. Which is worse for him? Losing a toy that he bought because he didn't pay back money he borrowed from you to buy it or having his car repossessed when he's in his twenties because he got behind on his payments? Teaching him well doesn't mean that he'll never make mistakes. It does, however, lessen the chances that he'll make those mistakes later in life.

This is a learning process for parents, too, and one of the biggest lessons we can learn is that we can't save people from themselves, even when we love them as much as we love our kids. We owe it to our children to give them a good financial foundation. The best foundation they can have is knowledge and confidence. One of the worst things we can teach them is that we'll always bail them out. The importance of this can't be stressed too much, so I'm going to keep saying it. Don't step in and "fix" every mistake your child makes. It leaves the parent in control rather than the child and can ultimately be more expensive for parents—both financially and emotionally. And this is an example of how we teach our kids by our actions, not just by our words.

Kids learn by example every day. Sometimes we're aware of it; sometimes we're not. Anyone who's been a parent realizes when a child is in a phase where he wants to be physically close to his parents all the time. Watch him during that phase and you'll see him put his hands in his pockets when his dad does or frown when his mom does. He'll do the same thing in watching how his family acts about money. Sometimes he might emulate his parents. Sometimes he might decide that he doesn't like the family's decisions and is going to avoid them. But parents show him the role money plays in their life just about every day. Let's look at a few examples.

Every day you come home and over dinner you tell your spouse that your job is a grind and your boss is an idiot. Your child hears this and, on some level, comes to the conclusion that working stinks. As a pre-schooler, she can't imagine why you torture yourself with this every day. As she gets older, she begins to pick up that this horrible thing you call work is necessary to get money and money is necessary to live. She might feel sorry for you and appreciate that you go through this level of self-sacrifice for her. Then comes the day that you suggest she needs to think about getting a job. How could you ask such a terrible thing of your own flesh and blood?

Everyone has bad days. And family is a primary support system, someplace to vent on these difficult days. So call your venting what it is—letting off steam on a bad day. There are good days too, and your children are drinking in what their family is showing them. Say that your job is usually a pleasant environment and you're grateful to have it.

But what if your job really does stink more often than not? Since this book is geared toward helping you teach your kids about money, this isn't the place to go into detail about the changes you need to make. But if that's how you feel, you need to see what would be involved in making some changes in your life and allow that process to teach your kids. If you are in a bad professional situation, at the very least, tell your kids that your situation is not what they should sign on for. They need to find something they enjoy doing and find out what careers will allow them to do that. It's better to build your financial life around what your dream career will allow you to earn than to build your career around what your lifestyle requires you to make. There's more on this in the chapter called Careers.

Let's look at another example. Every Tuesday night is Pay Bill Night. The entire household knows that on Tuesday nights, everyone is quiet and no one is allowed to bother you. Grunting and groaning noises come from you as you slam each bill on the table after you write the check to pay it. What are your kids learning? Bills are the bane of human existence. Having to deal with them is painful.

Let's turn that on its ear. You pay your bills every week and discuss them calmly with your spouse and sometimes even with your kids. If the long distance bill was a little high, discuss how it might be lowered and get their suggestions—don't just give out orders or reprimands. Let's say you've got a vacation coming up and you'd like to plan for it financially. Discuss it with the whole family and see how you can all save for it. Would everyone be willing to

- eat at home,

- cut back on movie outings, and
- save for their own spending money so the family can have a nice vacation and not need to pay it off for the rest of the year?

Here's another way you may be teaching when you don't realize it. You work hard, long hours. You don't mind because you love what you do for a living and you make money at it. Every time one of your kids has a game or a recital, you either can't make it, you're late, or you take several cell phone calls during the event. You are, however, a very good provider. You know your family appreciates the lifestyle you provide them. Every time you get a new car they all love or go on a great vacation, you remind them that all the hard work you do is what provides these great perks.

What we too often teach our kids when we have this approach is that getting lots of money is more important than time spent together or appreciating their accomplishments. They're learning that the role of work is to provide lots of money—not just enough for the basics. This is also an area where we can unintentionally turn our kids away from ourselves as an example. If the only thing your child wants is for you to get excited about her soccer match and watch an entire game without taking a phone call, she might decide that she doesn't want a demanding career. She wants a job that allows her to cover the financial basics, a home that's based on very minimal financial demands, and family time that's the only important focus in her life.

I have one memory from my middle school years that was an eye opener to me. I had a friend whose family, like mine, was lots of fun to be with. I guess I was aware that their house was smaller than ours and our cars were newer than theirs, but I was comfortable with them and my friend was comfortable with my family. One night I was spending the night with this friend, and her parents were both sitting at the kitchen table doing something. Her dad was writing periodically, and he and her mom would occasionally confer over some papers he had there. It was obvious that whatever they were doing was important, but they both seemed to be comfortable with it. I asked my friend what her parents were doing and she said, "They're paying bills." I think my response was some mixture of bewilderment and condolence. My folks never talked about household finances in front of me. It was like sex. It just wasn't discussed in polite company and never around the children. My friend sort of smiled and said, "It's fine. They do this every week." Okay. I knew there were some differences between us so maybe this was just another one of the things that were different from my family, but it seemed to be okay. My friend had already started to learn that bill paying is part of a happy life.

One of the best things you can do is discuss finances with your spouse and your kids. Some of these discussions can address your general outlook. For instance, if you use a credit card to pay for a dinner out with the family, while you're waiting to sign the receipt, talk about how credit cards work. Explain that it's important to pay them off each month so that you don't end up paying interest for months to come on purchases like the dinner the family just enjoyed. When you're finalizing plans for a big vacation, discuss how you already had the money saved and how saving up for big purchases and paying as you go means that over the long haul, you don't spend more than you make. Dad and Mom need to be the ultimate decision makers on most big financial issues. But your children can get huge benefits from being able to listen and to give their thoughts and have your response to their ideas. That means that when discussions are held, everyone's input is taken seriously and addressed. If your response is to laugh at or make derisive comments about your child's desire or point of view, it sends the message that some people—like you—know the right way to deal with money and others—your spouse, your kids, your neighbors—don't know how to deal with money. You may get several results you won't like.

- Arguments could become pretty common in this type of environment.
- Your child might shut down lines of communication, feeling that you're not going to listen so neither is he. He'll just wait until he's old enough to have his own money and then he can do with it what he wants.
- You might have convinced him that he isn't any good with money, so he'll go forward with a fear of making all the wrong decisions when he's in charge of his own money. If you allow your children to participate in your discussions about money, they'll begin to realize that money is something they can and should have control over. And they are a part of the family—a family that recognizes each financial choice has consequences.

As a financial planner, I have to watch myself to make sure that I don't discuss our money so much that it becomes an overemphasized issue. But when we need to get control of a family expense, we'll often tell the kids what it is and why we need to be more watchful. For instance, our family finds it entirely too easy to fall into the bad habit of eating dinner out too often. My husband and I both work, so meal planning and even grocery shopping sometimes fall through the cracks. We've shown our children how much it costs us in groceries to eat for a week and when we go out to eat, we'll let them see what the tab is. Whether it's a sit-down restaurant or fast food, feeding five people a meal out isn't cheap. When we start slipping toward eating out too much, it's as likely to be one of the kids saying that we need to eat at home as it is to be one of the adults. As our children have grown, they've even offered (without parental coercion) to help with meal planning and preparation.

Sometimes these discussions are more difficult if your children are involved. That doesn't mean you shouldn't include them, but it may make your financial processing more time-consuming and might even cause you to do some soul searching. Can't we eat at home for the rest of the year and have a better vacation? Why don't I get to have a car when you just spent four times what my car would cost on a luxury car? Why do I have to pay for college when you're putting all this money into your retirement account? How about if we stop paying for all these insurance policies and put that money toward a better house? Some of these issues are addressed in specific chapters in Part II. In all cases, you're going to have to give genuine answers that don't denigrate your child's thought process. And you might be pleasantly surprised how often your children come up with innovative solutions to some of your financial decisions.

This all leads eventually to how our personal, moral, religious, political, and other values affect our financial outlook. You probably know many people who were raised in one religion, but now are devout members of another faith. You also know people who were raised in one culture but now have enthusiastically chosen to live in a different one. It's the same with all values, including how people deal with money. Either intentionally or unintentionally, you'll convey your financial priorities to your kids. They might agree with your values and carry them forward in their adult lives. They might feel that your values had a negative effect on their childhood and ultimate outlook on life and they might choose different values. They might also find a way of approaching finance that suits their individual goals better than what they saw in your life. There can also be a combination of these results. Just remember, you are always teaching them, whether you intend to or not. Be aware of that fact and speak and act accordingly.

Even though talking about money falls pretty low in the ladder of effective teaching techniques, it can have a role. The first one is intertwined with teaching by example. Money is often one of those topics, like sex or religion, that people either refuse to discuss or they discuss so much you wish they'd shut up about it. With a healthy amount of discussion about money, your kids will learn from being included in financial conversations. I'm certainly not suggesting that you announce at the neighborhood barbeque what you made in wages last year, but families should be able to discuss their finances among themselves. Part of including your child in the discussion needs to be telling him that family financial matters are private and whatever is said is to be discussed only with the family. Besides giving your child insight into how you handle money, it conveys to your child that you trust him with this information and believe that he can understand it and, eventually, give input to the discussions.

Financial discussions will develop as your child's knowledge about money increases. For instance, your pre-schooler isn't going to be very interested in whether or not you refinance the house, but your high school or college kid might be. And the pre-schooler can begin to get a feel for finance when you discuss whether to go to a movie or to an amusement park for a fun outing. You'll want to be very careful what you discuss with your kids, especially until they're in about 4th or 5th grade. Younger children can learn from basic discussions of social outings, vacations, and toy purchases, but might be overwhelmed or frightened by talking about the mortgage or retirement planning. Too much discussion of family finances, especially the concept that you can't afford to do everything that pops onto the child's wish list, can cause the child anxiety about money. As harmless as, "Oh, honey, we can't afford that" sounds to an adult, to a pre-schooler, it can sound like, "We might lose our house and have to live in a box under a bridge." Instead of saying the family can't afford something, talk about what you have decided to purchase and why your decision makes more sense for your family. "That convertible is pretty, but our whole family can ride together in our car."

In the opportunities you offer your children around money—what they see you do and what you say—you are conveying a financial education that includes values.

- You might be teaching them that good people will always struggle with money.
- You might be conveying that money is top priority; do everything you can to get it and keep it.
- Perhaps the message is that money is bad.

Be sensitive to these perceived values when your children express them to you and make adjustments in the message you convey as you see fit. While you may think your child's perception is off, often perception becomes reality. If your child believes that money is more important to you than he is, that might be his experience. You teach him about money because you love him, not because you love money. That's a better experience for both of you.

Where Money Comes From

"If you would have your son to walk honorably through the world, you must not attempt to clear the stones from his path, but teach him to walk firmly over them—not insist upon leading him by the hand, but let him learn to go alone."
-Anne Bronte

A client told me a story once about a tough financial period in her life when her daughter was young. She didn't want to get the girl concerned about finances, but one day when the daughter asked for something, the mom had to tell her that they didn't have the money right now. The girl then asked, "Why don't you go to that machine and get some money? It always has money." Another client told me her memory of money when she was growing up and how it had influenced her decision to take control of her finances by working and saving. Her father died when she was quite young and her mother had inherited some money. She said whenever the family needed money, her mother would take the kids to the bank and she'd get into her safety deposit box and take out some coupons. The bank would then cash the coupons and the family would have money. One day, she said, there weren't any more coupons. The mother and her children went through some very lean and frightening times while she searched for work. She eventually did get a job, but she worked as long as she could and only had a meager check from social security after she wasn't able to work any more.

You owe your children the knowledge of where money comes from and how to handle it. During the time that your kids are at home, most of your money probably comes from a job. Most of the rest of the money people spend in their life comes from what they've saved and invested. Some children actually get enough money from gifts such as birthday and graduation to make that a major financial resource. Depending on your economic situation and the opportunities that come to your children, they need to understand how each of these items plays into your life and ultimately into their lives. This really is a two-fold process. One part is letting them know where their family's money comes from. The other part is letting them know where they can get money.

If you're like most Americans, most of your money comes the old-fashioned way—you or someone in the family earns it. Earning money doesn't have to be a horrible burden. Being out in the workforce can be fun and, for many people, a foundation for their social life. There's more about choosing a career in Part II. And one of the first financial concepts to expose a kid to is that she can get money when she does tasks or provides products that other people are willing to pay for. That's how her parents get money, so that can be a first exposure for her. Discussion here is essential. It's as important to get across to her what you enjoy about your job as it is to convey that that's where your money comes from. The concepts should be connected in your life and they should be discussed that way.

Investments will be the biggest piece of what supports most of us in retirement. To show your child that you are preparing for that is helpful, but usually not until he's in late middle school or high school. Until that time, it's not really a concept that has meaning for your child. Look at it this way. If you're 40 and your child is 10, you'll probably be saving for retirement for a period of time that's longer than he's been alive. You'll also be in retirement for a longer period than he's been alive. Until he gets a great sense of history and the future, retirement planning isn't going to click in his thinking. These concepts are discussed in more detail in Part II.

If a substantial portion of your money comes from another source—family money, a business that you sold, the lottery—the issues you deal with can be much more complex. Volumes can be written on financial education in such a situation. As a financial advisor, my approach is that even kids who may never have to budget or earn a living in their life should be given the same education about managing their money as people of average financial means. Children in this situation may also need additional education about managing wealth, but they still need to know how to earn money and spend it responsibly. There are several reasons for this. One is that there seems to be a lot of anecdotal evidence that people who come into a windfall—lottery winnings, inheritances, even large earnings from a business—frequently aren't able to keep the money. They spend it on items that make for a flashy lifestyle but are bad investments—fancy cars, vacations, drugs. Celebrities in a variety of industries—professional sports, movies, business—have exemplified unfortunate situations where sudden wealth is squandered or leads to excesses such as drug abuse and crime. Many of these people haven't had good financial education on how to handle this type of quick wealth and they're easy marks for people who put together money-losing investments. Lots of family and friends who want a loan show up after news about the money gets around, too, and lots of those loans are never repaid. Many who experience sudden wealth even end up in bankruptcy.

Another sad phenomenon is related to a phrase sometimes heard in the financial advisory industry. "Shirtsleeves to shirtsleeves in four generations." One generation earns money from the ground up, or close to it. They pass on a comfortable or even extravagant estate to the next generation. That next generation, the second one, knows the blood, sweat, and tears that their parents put into earning their wealth. These folks are good stewards of the money. Their children, the third generation, grow up with the assumption that money and comfort are the norm. Financial ease is an entitlement in their mind and not something that has to be earned or preserved. It's just there. Many of these people even have as a necessary part of their adult budget substantial and regular financial gifts from their parents, generation two. They might have a comfortable adult life or they might actually run out of money before they die. Their children, generation four, grow up in relative comfort, but they see their parents squander the family's financial resource. Generation four might even end up having to subsidize their once financially sound parents at some point. This last generation in the cycle begins it again. They are determined not to repeat the mistakes of their parents in having and losing money. They work hard, live below their means, and leave a financial estate to their children. And so the cycle has come full circle.

Financial education can be a key in stopping a dysfunctional cycle such as this. Even if your child's experience is that money comes from a trust fund or his inheritance, he'll stand a greater chance of maintaining his wealth if he's taught the basics of how the huddled masses get and manage their money.

Personal Notes

Choices, Relative Values, and Trade-Offs

"If you want your children to turn out well, spend twice as much time with them, and half as much money."
-Abigail Van Buren

I love movies, and one of my favorite scenes in our movie collection comes from "Rainman." Charlie, a cutthroat businessman, finds that he has a brother who is an autistic savant named Raymond. A doctor gives a basic explanation of Raymond's condition and Charlie jumps to the conclusion that Raymond is a genius. The doctor then asks Raymond how much a candy bar costs, to which Raymond replies that it costs about $100. The doctor then asks Raymond how much a car costs, to which Raymond replies that it costs about $100. Just about everyone has met someone who seems to have Raymond's feel for finance and many of us have suspected at one time or another that we are that person. Kids certainly start with this syndrome. There's no need to embarrass her, but I'm sure if you asked just about any grade-schooler how much her family's house cost, the answer would probably give you a good chuckle. There are several ways to give kids a better feel for how to compare things in terms of monetary values.

The first one is a sense of how much in earnings it takes to get something. This can be weeks of allowance or it can be hours of work or it can be a number of specific chores. For instance, if your middle-school-age daughter gets paid minimum wage for shredding papers at your office (like my kids do), she can be shown that the new hot music CD that she wants, which costs $14.95, will take just over three hours of shredding to buy. Let's take another scenario and throw in some alternatives. Let's say that you pay your grade-schooler $7 per week in allowance and there are some chores that he can do for money, but it's not required for him to do the chores. Assume that cleaning the toilet pays $2, mopping the floor pays $7, and vacuuming the living room pays $8. (All of these are bargains, if you ask me.) He has his eye on a new toy that costs $16. He has several choices if he wants to buy the toy. Wait for three weeks and have enough money from his allowance; wait for the week's allowance and either mop the kitchen or vacuum; mop, vacuum, and clean the toilet and have the toy before allowance is paid. I'm sure you could come up with some other scenarios, but you get the idea.

Having these alternatives already in place in your family makes it an easy opening to discuss money. When your child comes to you and says she wants a new doll, first let her know that it's something that you'd expect her to pay for. Then ask how much it costs. Then start working through the alternatives she has for getting that much money. The process is basically the same, although the purchase and alternatives change, as the child grows older. At some point, your older children may talk through with you what they want to buy and how they want to buy it. Or they might even just tell you the plan, without asking for input.

The next step in understanding relative values is deciding between alternatives. For instance, if your child wants to go to a concert that costs $25 and to buy a new shirt that costs $25, but he's only got $30, he has some alternatives. One decision might be to either buy the shirt or go to the concert. He basically decides whether he'd rather have a shirt he can wear for a while or have the experience of attending this particular concert. One conclusion, which might be less than fully conscious on his part, is that the shirt and the concert are of the same value. Subsequent decisions might include whether or not to work additional hours at his job so he could do both. He might decide that his leisure time is worth more to him than having both.

This type of understanding can come very early. Would your child like to have a swim party or laser tag for her birthday? She won't be able to have both, but the costs are comparable. Would she rather get the doll or the toy car with her allowance and chore money? Don't let this thought process lead to a sense of lack or limitation. It's not about what the child can't have. It's about being able to choose what she'd rather have from among the acceptable alternatives.

The next concept is a bit more complex and will probably have to wait until your child gets older. That's the difference between needs and wants. As adults, we make this decision pretty regularly, even if it's not on a conscious level. For instance, you need shelter. You don't need a five-bedroom house with a great view in a gated community, but that's what you want. You need transportation to and from your job. You don't need a sassy sports car, but you want a cool car. You need food. You don't need to eat at a nice restaurant, but you want to have a rest from cooking every once in a while. Each of these wants can be legitimate and it's your decision to make the financial commitment to those things rather than having the need they fulfill met in a more Spartan way.

Probably all of what your younger children (up through middle school) will spend their own money on falls into the want category. That's a healthy approach. After all, you don't want your child growing up with memories of childhood that suggest that he was a child slave so that his basic needs could be met. As children get older, into the mid and late teens, some of the money they earn along with money you provide them for discretionary spending can go to meet needs such as clothing and transportation. You can, at that point, show the difference between needs and wants by pointing out the financial differences.

If your daughter needs new school clothes, do some comparative shopping with her and show her what generic brand or even used clothes cost compared to new designer labels. She can have the same number of outfits for less with less expensive clothes, she could get more outfits for the same amount she'd spend on a few high dollar pieces, or she can buy a few high priced outfits that she can mix and match for the look she wants. If the amount of money to spend is the same, the lesson is there to be learned. And this is where it may be difficult for you to let her develop her own values. You might find it wasteful that she'd spend so much on one outfit. You also might find her look to be less than satisfactory if she goes the inexpensive route. You can point out where you disagree, but she needs to make the decision. And the consequences for that decision shouldn't come from you, they should come from her experience. If she goes with expensive clothes and fewer outfits, that's more effective than you telling her that you refuse to continue helping her with her laundry if she spends her clothing budget that way. This is her choice and she's building the wardrobe she wants, not the one you want.

These choices and distinctions with needs and wants extend to lots of areas of your child's life—transportation, jobs, college, and more. In some cases you may have to come up with some creative ways to have input without forcing a decision on your child. Let's say you and your son did all the college visits and applications. You were both pleased that he got accepted to an exclusive private college and you are going to be able to pay for that education. Now he says that instead of going to that college, he'd like to start at the local junior college and finish at the state university that's 100 miles from home. He proposes that you pay him the difference in the cost of the private school and what his plan will cost. What's your reply? Would your reply be different if he said he'd use the money you give him to fund his own business when he's finished with college? What if he said he'd use the money you give him to go to law school?

It's imperative that you remember that your child needs to be learning to make his own decisions—in all aspects of his life—and live with the outcomes. Your child isn't a chance for you to live your life over, either to duplicate your great decisions or to make up for your bad ones. A good public college education along with the trip to Europe for a year may be the best life experience that he could have. And if you hadn't planned on paying for law school, his ability to go without having too much in student loans might be a wonderful solution. You can also build in some safety nets without completely usurping his decision. For instance, you might say that you retain control of the college funds until he has graduated. Or you might give him some of the money each summer for travel if his grades during that school year meet predetermined levels. In this scenario, we're talking about your money, so it's reasonable to outline how it will be used. You still shouldn't use the money—or any money—as a weapon or manipulation tool.

There may be some instances where you feel that your child can't be allowed to make a bad decision because the repercussions last a lifetime and he can't possibly see that at this point in his life. There will be some instances where his personal safety or long term future dictate that you make a decision for him. But don't use that as a rationalization for making all of his decisions. Even some of the big ones need to be made by him. If you send him to an expensive college and he flunks out, who does that benefit? Or what if he graduates from that expensive college with a degree in a lucrative field that he hates? Whose interests are served by that?

As children grow into adults, they need the encouragement to let their individuality develop without making mistakes that can mar their future. Some of what your child wants to do will be unwise and you need to set up a system where unwise decisions can't do permanent harm, but where a lesson can be learned. This system will allow the child to make very small decisions initially. As she gets more comfortable with making her decisions and she has had some good results from her choices, you can let her make more important and bigger financial decisions. Often you can ask questions about how a decision might turn out instead of giving advice. For instance, asking, "Do you think that toy is going to last very long?" can be more effective and less intrusive on her autonomy than saying, "That toy is just a cheap piece of junk! It'll break before you can play with it twice." When a mistake occurs, it's very important to have a loving, supportive discussion without blame. It's much better for you to say, " I'm sorry that the toy you bought broke before you'd had it for very long," instead of "I told you that toy was a piece of junk!" And don't offer to "make it all better" by reimbursing her for the broken toy or buying her a new one. If you think the product was faulty, you can offer to go with her to the store to see about a refund or replacement if she's too young to do it alone or if she's never had to make a similar complaint. You also need to recognize when your child is making a good decision that's simply different from what you would choose.

A Bright Leitz Money Map Book

Personal Notes

Setting Parameters

"It is frequently said that children do not know the value of money. This is only partially true. They do not know the value of your money. Their money, they know the value of."
- Judy Markey

We've all seen parents who made the mistake of having no rules for their children when they were young and trying to impose increasing discipline as the children got older. That's not a very effective way to parent. If children are given limited choices when they are young along with immediate feedback on what isn't acceptable, they get used to making workable choices. Then when they enter some of their more challenging growing periods—gotta' love teenagers, it's the only way to adulthood—they are better equipped to make wise choices and it's less likely that the parents have to put strict rules in place. It's the same with money. If young kids get a feel for what it is to make some small decisions with money, they'll be better able to make good financial decisions when the stakes are higher.

When your child is very young—preschool through elementary school—you'll want to set the boundaries for the use of money very clearly. As the child gets into late elementary and early middle school, the acceptable uses can be more broadly defined. When your child gets into high school, you are likely to find that the foundation you've laid with money means that you'll only have to respond to specific situations. Let's look at how it can all work.

Your child's first exposure to money will probably be through an allowance, which can happen as early as 5 or 6 years old. There are more details on how to structure this in the chapter about allowance in Part II of the book. Before money ever hits the child's pocket, discuss with him what he can use the money for and have it be as specific as possible. Toys, snacks at the mall, candy, an extra trip to McDonald's. You know what the child will probably want to use the money for. Also, begin using empowering language with him about the money. Talk about it as "his money," not just money that you give him. In terms of options, you can be as broad as to say that his money will be for things that you don't intend to buy for him, but—and this is very important—he's not allowed to spend his money on anything that you wouldn't allow him to have. Knives, boa constrictors, a motorcycle. Then tell him the consequences of buying something that you won't allow him to have. You can customize this for your situation, but one of the most effective consequences is that if he buys something that you prohibit, you take the purchase from him and he's not reimbursed for the cost. In other words, he loses both the contraband item and what it cost him to buy it. Your circumstances might allow him to return the item, if it's in returnable condition, but he has to go with you to where he purchased it and go through the return process. When your child is quite young, that will probably not be an issue. Many of the "illegal" items will be things like candy or inappropriate stickers. Rather than have the child play a guessing game as to whether his purchase will pass muster with you, let him know up front that he's always welcome to ask you before he buys something. Initially, this might leave you feeling that you're making all the purchase decisions. But as your child gets comfortable with what he is and isn't allowed to use his money for, he'll phase you out of the purchase approval mode.

Just about everyone who's given a bit of latitude makes a few mistakes. So your child will probably make some poor choices during his financial education. The easy thing to do—for both of you—is to bail him out. Don't do it! He needs to face the outcome of a bad decision. Even early in the child's life, there are some pretty effective financial traps. Magazine subscriptions, music and video clubs, cheap toys. If he gets a magazine subscription that just doesn't stop coming, make sure he deals with it. Tell him what his options are: write a letter stopping the subscription, report them to the Better Business Bureau, return the magazines. But don't do it for him. If he asks for your help, you may decide to help, but don't take the problem out of his hands. He's much more likely to remember the lesson if he does it himself. It's heartbreaking to have your child spend money on a cheaply made toy that ends up broken within days. But don't offer to replace or pay for it. His lesson of personal responsibility is better learned if you don't. This lesson is also less expensive now than when your child is a young adult buying high dollar items like cars or a house. Learning the lesson that hard way when he's young is much less expensive than making the same mistake later in life.

Remember that the child can make a valid decision that doesn't match the decision you would make. He can choose to buy more trendy clothes and have fewer of them. You may have to come to grips with the more difficult realization that you can't save some people from themselves. Each of us has to ultimately make our own decision and live with it. Your child might make some very unwise decisions now and for many years to come. If this is the case, one of the key facts you establish is that you are not going to save him from his bad decisions. Too many parents make all their child's financial decisions for them. They don't let the child experiment with finding his own money personality and priorities. Then when the child is a teenager or young adult, he makes a big expensive mistake and the parents come to the rescue. The parents pay off debt or pay for whatever is needed. The "lesson learned" includes a stern lecture on good financial management and, often, a warning that the child won't be rescued again. But when the next mistake happens, the parents step in again to help with the financial emergency. The true lesson being learned is "Whenever things go wrong, my parents will step in and fix it." This is an expensive and bad lesson. It keeps your child from being on his own and it can jeopardize your financial soundness. If less expensive mistakes are made by the child at a young age without you saving the day, the chances are much better that the child will be able to financially make it on his own. It also makes for a child that you might find much more interesting as an adult. He's going to learn some things that you might enjoy learning from him.

What if your child is already in high school or college and you realize that he needs some financial education? It's always easier to teach life skills at an early age, but it's never too late. The basic approach can be similar to starting with a younger child. Give the child several acceptable alternatives to choose from in how to approach a financial decision and let him decide. Then let him live with the results of his choice.

It may be that he makes a choice that you didn't give him and that you don't approve of. He needs to deal with the results of that choice. And if you're providing the money for the choice, some results might be that you either ask to be reimbursed or that you don't provide money that he was expecting from you for something else. However you structure the learning experience, it's important that you resist the temptation to do a bail out.

For instance, if your child has a clothing budget and he spends a huge amount of it on a leather jacket but doesn't buy underwear or socks, let him live with the consequences. He'll learn much more from having to do laundry every night so he has clean boxers and socks than if you buy those items for him to help him out.

Personal Notes

Using Money for Enforcement

"If you want to recapture your youth, just cut off his allowance."
— Al Bernstein

Many parents feel that money is a great way to bring about desired results. I'd have to disagree and caution against money as an enforcement tool. Probably your child learns most effectively through her own experience and through your example. Using money to modify behavior can have the very negative effect that the child thinks everything is about money. Even some good uses of money for enforcement can turn negative if they're not presented in the proper light. Let's look at some examples.

You're trying to work at home one evening and the kids are being so loud that you can't concentrate. Finally you go to the kids and say that you'll pay them each $5 an hour to be quiet. That financial consequence just doesn't have any bearing to what goes on in reality. There are virtually no jobs where people get paid just for not being loud. There may be other ways to bring about the desired effect that may or may not involve money. Maybe they need to clean their rooms and now would be a good time for that to get accomplished. Or maybe there's a project that you'd be willing to pay the kids for, like cleaning the kitchen, that would be relatively quiet, keep them busy for a good amount of time, and you'd be willing to pay a maid to do the same work. Maybe there's even something that they can do to help you, like putting the bills and checks in their envelopes or helping to sort the closet with you—something that would have the kids quietly involved in what you're doing. Don't rule out that they might just need to be quiet because they're supposed to be quiet. And the only positive consequence of staying quiet might be that they're not required to go to bed early or stay alone in their rooms.

Grades seem to be a popular item for families to reward monetarily. I know parents and extended family members that pay kids for each A they get in school. Think through the logic to this strategy. You want your children to do well in school so they can get a good job. So if you pay them for good grades, they start to associate excelling in their daily activities, which right now center around school, with making money. So far so good. Some people who are academically oriented are paid quite well, have good financial benefits from their jobs, and have financial security. But it's not always a direct consequence of their good grades. Money for grades can work for many families and help the kids see some positive reward from their grades in addition to the feeling of accomplishment. We generally reward academic achievement in our family more with experiences like an evening out with the parents or a later bedtime.

Charging kids money as a punishment can be a slippery slope. While it might get their attention, it might send the message that you—not they—control their money. There are some times when taking money from your child can be a logical consequence. At one point all three of our kids were taking piano lessons. The piano teacher came to our house once a week and they each got their lesson. One of the children was bored with piano and didn't pay attention during the lesson. One week when I noticed this was a problem, I interrupted the lesson to tell the child that if she continued to waste the lesson time, she'd have to pay back to her father and me what the lesson cost. The teacher heard the exchange and the rest of that lesson went pretty well. The following week, though, when I asked the teacher how the lessons went, she said that particular child had been horsing around instead of paying attention. I went to the child and told her the report the teacher had given on her. The lessons cost $9 each and her savings at that point were about $27. I told her very specifically that it was too bad that her poor behavior took her savings from $27 down to $18, but that it wasn't fair to her dad and me to pay for lessons that she was wasting. It worked. She was well-behaved and attentive in her lessons after that.

Perhaps the biggest pitfall about using money for enforcement is having money overemphasized with your child. Everyone's life has many facets, each of which needs to stay in perspective. They'll have lessons to learn about academics, making friends, religion, health, and much more. It all needs to be in the proper balance. Having your child get paid when he's good and get charged a fee when he's bad gives money more of a role than it deserves in his life. Also, it sets a foundation to have you control your child through money. That's highly dysfunctional for both of you.

Personal Notes

Getting Started

"Wise mothers and fathers rebuke and praise just to the right degree."
- Dr. Frank Crane

Here are the points that you'll want to keep in mind as you embark on this educational journey.

- When you are teaching children about money, give them a few alternatives for how to earn and spend the money. All the choices need to be ones that you're okay with.
- Respect the individuality your kids express with their financial decisions. It's not important that they make decisions you would make. It's important that they learn to make their own choices and live with the consequences.
- Don't bail them out of bad financial decisions. Many people learn best from their own experiences. When they are young, the mistakes are less expensive and more likely to change future behavior than later in life. If you do bail them

out, you're teaching them that you'll always be there to save them.

- The hardest lesson for you may be that you can't save people—even the ones you love the most—from themselves. Allowing children the opportunity to learn from their own experiences while they're young lessens the chance they'll need saving later in life.

Part II of this book gives you some ideas on specific strategies you can use. Not every lesson works for every child. Feel free to use the ideas here, but make sure your radar is picking up on what will work best with your kids.

Personal Notes

PART TWO

Allowance

"Don't bite the hand that has your allowance in it."
-Paul Dickson, quoting a youngster named Lois

Receiving an allowance will be the first experience most children have in actually having their own money and making decisions about how to spend it. There are three major components in structuring a child's allowance:

(1) how much he gets,

(2) what restrictions he has on spending it, and

(3) the age at which he starts getting it.

It may be a good idea to ask your friends and your child's friends' parents about these items. Make sure, however, that you have a sense of what those other children are allowed to spend their money on and what that family spends their money on. Don't try to keep pace with the big spenders you know. If you believe it's not ideal for a child to grow up with a passion for designer clothes and fancy cars, you might not want to follow the example of a family who wears and drives only the most expensive choices. Lastly, decide how often allowance should be paid. All these factors will change as the child grows. How the allowance evolves and how you discuss it and the purchases your child makes with it can be some of the most valuable financial educational tools you have.

When a child gets allowance depends on several factors. There are some basic financial concepts about money that you should be introducing to your child through your example and through discussion. The first examples and discussions are going to involve comparable value and the concept that money is not limitless. If your child is asking you what he can choose from when shopping or asking if you and he can spend money on lunch or some other item while out, he's probably ready to receive an allowance. Some children as young as 5 or 6 can start appreciating the ability to have money they can use for themselves and not waste the opportunity.

How much a child gets is the first big decision for a parent to make and there are many right approaches to this decision. A good rule of thumb is that a child can be responsible for $1 per week for every year of their age. In other words, $6 per week would be a reasonable allowance for a 6-year-old child. If you have two or three children and they are all very close in age, you may want to give all the children the same amount each week and give them raises of the same amount at the same time. There may be other factors that affect how much allowance to give your child. Usually the biggest one is what the child will use the money for.

Before a child receives allowance, decide what he will be allowed to spend it on and tell him the range of choices. There's no doubt that he will ask if he can buy something (or just buy it) that it never occurred to you to exclude from the list of acceptable purchases, but thinking through it ahead of time will help you and him understand the acceptable criteria for spending. It's also a good idea to give some general conceptual guidelines in addition to any specific guidelines.

For instance, you can introduce the allowance to your child by saying that you will be paying him $6 a week and he can use it to buy things he wants like

- toys,
- candy,
- a treat at the school cafeteria, or
- a meal at the mall while shopping instead of waiting to eat at home.

He needs to understand, however, that you won't allow him to spend the money on something dangerous or to have or do something that he knows you don't want him to do. You can give a list of things you won't allow, whether it's

- tattoos,
- piercings,
- music with profanity, or
- whatever is inappropriate from your perspective,

or you can give him some more general parameters—anything that's against your values. If he uses the money for something that is against your wishes, you will not allow him to keep his purchase, so he will have lost that money. It would be best to give some unacceptable examples so that he understands the parameters. Also, allow him to be able to ask you if something is an unacceptable purchase and encourage him to ask when he's in doubt.

It's very important that you realize that this is an opportunity for the child to learn to make his own responsible decisions with money.

These decisions may differ greatly from the decisions you would make. If he wants to buy a green shirt and you want him to buy the shirt in red, he will learn from the ability to "put his money where his mouth is" and say he'll buy the green shirt with his own money. This is different from him buying a shirt with gang symbols or profanity on it, which would be a purchase that he would forfeit to you.

As the child matures, both the allowance and its uses can be expanded. In the mid teens, most children can begin having their allowance include their clothing budget. It's a good idea to initially say how much the allowance is increasing to allow for clothes. For instance, if you increase your son's allowance from $15 a week to $50 a week, make sure to say that $35 of that is intended for clothing. As part of the child's process of learning to work with the consequences of monetary decisions, he may make some choices that deviate from the budget you had in mind. Your son may decide to go to a concert with his increased allowance rather than have new clothes for school. He might also decide not to buy a stereo he's wanted because he wants to buy a new ski jacket. Another item that can be incorporated into allowance is school lunch money. Be sure, however, that you are willing to let your child go without lunch if he doesn't budget properly.

During the teens is usually a good time to extend the time between allowance payments from weekly to bi-weekly or even monthly. When a child is younger, he's more likely to spend money as soon as he gets it. Over time he'll develop his ability to make money last, even past the next time he's paid. For instance, you might pay your 13- year-old every other week and start paying him monthly when he turns 16. Obviously the allowance gravy train should stop at some point. Terminating allowance will depend on what you've decided and discussed with your child about what he does after high school. If he's going to college, he should be responsible for his spending money at a minimum. See the Education Funding chapter for more detailed ideas. If he's going to get a job out of high school, he should be responsible for his living expenses—gas and insurance for his car, food, something toward rent and utilities—even if he's living with you.

Many people disagree on whether or not allowance should be tied to household chores. Some people feel that chores are part of being in a family and should be done whether or not the child gets allowance. Others feel that allowance for chores introduces the concept of earning money as well as responsibility at home. Valid arguments can be made either way. If you tie allowance to chores, be consistent about it. Each child should be given specific chores and know how his allowance will be affected if he doesn't do chores. If the chores aren't done, don't pay the allowance. Ideally, allowance isn't increased for extra household duties unless the tasks are ones you'd pay someone outside the home to do. If you choose not to pay for chores, be careful that you don't suggest that a full time homemaker has no value. In our society, which often puts too much emphasis on money, no monetary value too often suggests no value.

At one point, our family went from a regular allowance without specific duties attached, to having the kids only be paid for specific household chores. We made a list of specific duties that a maid might do. We assigned a price to each chore and made a master list of what constituted completing the duty. For instance, the chore of Cleaning the Master Bathroom included vacuuming the carpet, scrubbing the shower and the sinks, cleaning the mirror (without any streaks), cleaning the toilet (always a big hit), and wiping down the counters. Each child had to sign up for an equal number of chores and have them completed by 6:00 p.m. each Saturday. If a chore wasn't completed on time, the child still had to finish it, but wasn't paid for the work. If my husband or I didn't feel that the work was satisfactory, we'd give specifics on what was wrong and have the child correct it. If the kids wanted to swap out chores and make a financial arrangement between themselves, that was allowed. We didn't give anyone a week off, though. This worked for us for several reasons. Prior to this arrangement, the kids weren't realizing the impact of their messiness. We were constantly having them stop what they were doing to clean up messes. With the new system, the house didn't have a professionally cleaned appearance all the time, but the kids started reminding each other to clean up since they took pride in their work and they realized if someone made a mess, they might have to clean it up during the next week.

A family told me that they pay each of their kids an allowance and each has chores. As soon as each child is paid, he has to pay taxes, rent, utilities, and food to the parents. This may seem too harsh for some. The father told me, though, that it's very satisfying to see his grade school age daughter tell his teenage son to stop leaving the light on when he leaves a room because he's costing her money.

It can also be effective to include some minimum requirements for what is done with allowance. Some people feel that they learned to save by being required to save a set amount from each allowance. Others were required to put part in savings and part in the church collection and allowed to spend the rest. Such a plan can develop a sense of charitable giving as well as a saving mentality. Part of the potential downfall with these required uses of allowance is that they take away some of the child's discretion regarding money. If the point of giving him allowance is to have him make decisions, making some of the initial usage decisions for them can defeat the purpose of the allowance to a certain extent.

Paying allowance in a regular and timely way is a good pattern to set. Paying at the same time every week or month gives the child a sense of budgeting and what it's like to get a regular paycheck. Paying each allowance on time begins to instill a sense of responsibility. If you pay allowance late, it may give the child an idea that he can pay things late, too—like bills.

There are a couple of related areas that are dealt with in more detail in later chapters. Your child will occasionally receive cash gifts from friends and family. This is addressed in detail in the chapter Gifts. Another issue that relates to allowance is borrowing. Your child may ask for an advance on allowance. Look at the chapter Debt Used Wisely for tips on this.

Your child will make some mistakes with his allowance. It's much easier to make mistakes with money and learn the underlying lessons as a child than as an adult. Do not bail out your child when he makes a mistake! It may be more painful for you to watch your child suffer over the error than it is for him. He'll be less likely to make a similar mistake in the future if you don't rescue him. Remember, you're often teaching by your actions—often more than by your words—whether you intend to or not. If you always save him from financial loss, you're teaching him that you're going to fix every mistake he makes. When he's an adult, that will be more expensive than now—for you and for him.

Personal Notes

Bargains

"A fool and his money are soon parted."
- English proverb

We all know some unfortunate soul who is basically a shopaholic. He thinks he saves $30 when he sees a $100 item that he doesn't need is marked down to $70, so he buys it. He just can't see that he didn't save anything. He blew $70! That's not a bargain. Getting a bargain is buying something that you need or would like to have and getting a price on it that's less than you would have been willing to pay. Developing the Bargain Hunting Mentality is more an art than a science. And for some people, it's a bona fide passion.

My three children got their first stereos at pretty young ages. My son was about 9 and had seen a stereo at a wholesale store where we shopped regularly that carried everything from rice to TVs to tires. He saw a nice little unit that had a CD player, tape player, an AM/FM radio, and speakers that could be placed as much as six feet away from the unit. It wasn't exactly the beginning of a high-end component system, but for $129, it looked really good to a 9-year-old. We talked with him at length about how much $129 is—how many weeks' allowance and how many hours of work at Mom's office that translates to. He was smitten and knew that he'd be willing to pay more to get the stereo and could also see from an area electronics store that if he didn't buy the unit at the wholesale store before they ran out, he would pay more. It only took him a few weeks to save the money.

The whole thing seemed pretty uninteresting to his two sisters until we actually took the unit home and put it in his room. Suddenly both of them wanted stereos in their rooms. But they didn't have nearly that much saved. About a month later an electronics store had a sale on some low-end stereos. A unit with a CD player and an FM radio was running around $35, which fit within their budgets. These units weren't nearly as nice as their brother's in either the sound quality or the features, but all three kids were stereo- satisfied at that point. Each girl had a stereo she could listen to in the privacy of her room. Our son had a much nicer stereo that would last a long time and get great use. All three were happy and all three had their first experience with a bargain.

Bargain hunting can become more sophisticated as your child gets older and is involved in purchasing more expensive items. Buying something inexpensive that's poorly made can be more expensive in the long run. If, however, your child knows that he'll only wear a shirt he's buying for one season, a cheap price for cheap quality might be okay. Looking for end-of-season closeout sales can be a good source of inexpensive, quality items. One woman has developed the habit of taking her teenage daughter shopping for her fall homecoming dress in the late spring or early summer. They've saved as much as 80% of the original cost. When your child gets benefits from saving money—in the form of getting to have money left to spend on other things—he may start getting excited about bargains. Resale shops, e-bay, generic brands, and stores that sell slightly irregular items may become quite popular around your house.

An expensive purchase is a great opportunity to have your child learn about bargains and quality. A prime example is his first car. Before a purchase is made, he needs to research

- insurance costs,
- safety,
- resale, and
- maintenance costs,

at a minimum. Even with a used car, information is available on the model and now there are services that may be able to provide the history of a specific vehicle. If you will be making any kind of financial contribution to this purchase, you can make such research a requirement. You won't make your contribution until he's satisfied you on the points that are important to you. If he's paying for the entire thing, you can suggest that he research it, but it's going to be his decision.

One excellent way to avoid impulsive non-bargain buying is to never give allowance immediately before a shopping trip. Most of us know that if we go to the grocery store hungry we'll buy more than we need. The same type of effect can happen with some of us if we go shopping when we feel flush with cash. That being said, if your child has saved long and hard for a particular purchase, it can give him a great sense of satisfaction and accomplishment to go straight to the store the instant he gets the last bit of money that makes him able to make the purchase. This can be an event you want to support.

Bargain hunting is the opposite of impulse buying. That can be helpful for you to remember when giving your child the opportunity to develop the Bargain Hunting Mentality. If you're at the mall and your child sees something he instantly falls in love with, tell him that you can come back and look at it again if he wants to at the end of the outing. Also, if he doesn't have his own money with him, do not lend him the money to buy it and let him pay you back when you get home. Part of being a wise shopper is buying only what you have the money to buy. When you're young and you have your spendable money in cash, you need to have the cash with you to buy something. Also, this shouldn't turn into a major inconvenience for you. If he doesn't have the money with him, taking him home to get his money and bringing him back doesn't teach him anything. It's just a pain for you. Ultimately, though, your child is going to buy some things or pay some prices that you think are unwise. When this happens, remember that this is not about teaching him to put your desires about money into practice. It's about letting him figure out what's important to him about money. Either way, it removes the burden to fulfill your children's financial whims.

Budgeting

"Gives me some kind of content to remember how painful it is sometimes to keep money, as well as to get it."
- Samuel Pepys

Most adults shudder or roll their eyes when you mention budgeting. So how on earth can you get your children interested in this dry topic about a restriction that no one seems to like to deal with? First, don't see it as a restriction. We all know that we can't have everything we set our eyes on. Budgeting is simply deciding what our priorities are and structuring our financial situation accordingly. You might find it helpful to call it something other than budgeting, like spending design or money planning. The concept is the important thing and a rose by any other name....

When younger children want something that costs more than their regular weekly allowance, talk with them about how long they need to save to get it—keeping in mind that before the age of eight, a goal of longer than three or four weeks is pretty hard to stick to. Let's say that your 6-year-old son gets $6 a week and wants to buy a plastic truck that costs $10. You can explain to him that if he saves his allowance for two weeks, he can buy the truck. Set up a place where he can keep the money he's saving. It can be a jar, a wallet, a box, or anything else that will work for him and you. The nice thing about a wallet or something comparable is the advantage of being convenient to bring along when a purchase is made. A jar or box has the advantage of being a little less accessible. A clear jar actually lets him see the money accumulating. You and your child can talk about what makes most sense. Whatever type of container you and the child choose, it can be in his room or it can be in a space that you control. If you decide on a space that you control, don't allow yourself to begin making his financial choices for him. However, if he gets distracted from his goal of purchasing the truck, you will have the opportunity to discuss his choice and the consequences of the choice before he spends the money.

If he sees a comic book that he wants in the first week that costs $3, remind him that if he buys the comic, he won't have the $10 he needs next week to buy the truck. Then—and this is very important—let him make the decision whether or not to buy the comic. If he buys the comic and later complains about not being able to have the truck, remind him of his choice. Take the opportunity to discuss with him whether having the comic was worth not having the truck.

If he holds out and saves for the truck, this may be an instance where you want to head for the truck store as soon as he gets his second week of allowance. He's had to show self-control in saving for a couple of weeks. Being able to get what he's saved for as soon as he has the money can be good reinforcement for budgeting. Besides sharing in his excitement at the new toy, tell him how proud you are that he had the self-control to budget and save for something he wanted. Another good way to show your support of his accomplishment is to tell his friends or his friends' parents how he got the toy.

As kids get older, say from about 9 to 13, the amount of time they can budget for gets longer. When your child is in her mid teens, she may be ready to have her allowance increased to cover some of the basic things you provide for her, such as clothes. Before you give her control of that budget, make sure you go over with her what the money is to cover. If she's given a clothing budget, it needs to include some mundane things like underwear and socks, not just trendy shirts and pants. And if she has to have other clothes, like a good dress for special occasions, make sure that she knows that has to be included in the budget. Before turning the clothing budget over to her, you may want to have her do some research on what her clothes will cost. This can be done several ways. One would be to go shopping for clothes together, but not buy anything. Make a list of what she needs. At the store, put the price of each item beside it on the list. If her list is beyond the budget you've allotted for clothes, ask her questions about where she would make adjustments to come in under budget. Once you've actually turned the money over to her, be prepared to let her deal with the consequences. If she gets a great new shirt but has to wear underwear with holes in it, let her deal with the holes. Also, if she blows the clothing budget on a great pair of earrings, let her wear the earrings with high-water pants and old shirts. As with allowance, make sure she knows what you consider an unacceptable purchase and give her the ability to get your approval for any purchases that might not be okay with you. If she buys something that you will not allow her to have, she loses the item and you don't reimburse her for it.

It's okay to remind your child to allow for some of the big things that might lie ahead in the foreseeable financial future. There are some events in our kids' lives that have run completely out of control financially. If they had to include in their budget (instead of assuming that we'd cover it) a prom dress, limo, flowers, and dinner at the most expensive restaurant in town, they might find some less expensive ways to celebrate. While it's reasonable to give some financial gifts when memorable life events occur, going along without some limit on costs at these times can destroy much of the work you and your children have accomplished about learning to be financially responsible. They must understand that money is not limitless.

Allowing teen-agers an allowance that includes items such as clothing, gasoline, and school lunches gives them the opportunity to start planning for some living expenses and balancing the cost of necessities with the cost of discretionary purchases. This makes them better prepared to deal with the independence they'll have at college or in their first apartment. If the first time your child has to make decisions about how much to pay for clothes is when she's on her own working and paying rent in her first apartment, she could end up making some pretty expensive mistakes.

The budgeting process can be a creative outlet for your child. Finding what motivates her can make it fun for her and you. You might have a story about something that you really wanted to include in your own budget that you can share. If she's an organizer, ask her if she could design a form that you could each use to set a budget each month and see how your actual spending compares to your plans. A friend once said to me that he found a budget very liberating. When he didn't have a budget, he never knew if he was spending too much and he was nervous about every penny. When he was on a budget, he always felt content with everything he spent because he knew it was in the budget.

Careers

"To twice think in every matter and follow the lead of others is no way to make money."
- Ihara Saikaku

There is a major difference between a job and a career. For kids, a job is something you do for money. They don't need to have a huge overwhelming drive or passion about it. They just need to be conscientious about fulfilling the duties involved. A job is often not something that's going to be a long-term career.

Just about everyone eventually has to support himself with a job. My opinion is that long-term personal financial success is better achieved if someone loves what he does for a living. If you agree with this, the best approach is for your child to figure out what he loves—in school or as a hobby—and find out what kind of careers he can have doing that and what those careers pay. Entirely too many people approach this decision from the other end of the equation. "What jobs pay lots of money? Lawyers? I could be a lawyer!" Then they spend lots of time and money going to law school and getting hired by a big law firm. They hate the hours, they hate the work, they hate the clients, and they hate the other lawyers. This doesn't mean that all lawyers hate what they do. Many of them are passionate about their work, love their clients, and make plenty of money doing it. But what makes them good at it and keeps them in that career is that they love it. It's not just about the money. The point is that we all spend too much time making a living to hate our jobs. We have a choice in it and should make a decision about what we do, rather than just stumbling into something to make a living and then being stuck because of the lifestyle we need to support. In the best of situations, a career is a long-term series of jobs that allows someone to pursue activities about which she can feel passionate and fulfilled. If your child can find that in her life, she's more likely to be able to have a fulfilling life than if she has chosen a career predominantly because of how much money she can make.

Even when your child is in elementary school, if she expresses interest in someone's job, look for opportunities to have her see what that job entails. As she gets older, you might help her see if she can get informational interviews with or articles about people whose jobs interest her. Also, look at her favorite subjects in school. Work with her to find career paths in fields that utilize those subjects. Putting a career in this positive perspective helps make earning a living an affirmative force in her life, not a financial burden.

The healthiest balance between career and money is to have your child find something that she loves to do and make a living at it. Even if she isn't making as much money as she could, she won't dread going to work every day and she won't be counting the days until she can retire. As a financial planner, I regularly hear people say that they'll never retire. Unfortunately, some of them are saying it because they realized too late in life that they needed to save for retirement and now they don't believe they can save enough. Most of them, though, love what they do and don't want to sever their ties with that activity. If your child can find what motivates her like that, she'll be happy with her career choice and have a higher likelihood of being willing to find a lifestyle that can be supported by that career. This lifestyle choice is supported by the career choice, too. Many of us make some of our best friends through the workplace. The effect can often be having most of our social exposure to people that are in the same general financial situation that we are. We might read about or know through some other avenues people who make much more than we do, but most of the people we see every day live in a house that's about what we can afford, drive a car that's comparable to ours, and vacation in the places we can afford to go. That's why choosing a career strictly for the money can be such a trap. If you have developed a lifestyle that requires a certain level of income, you probably feel that you can't consider a less lucrative career because you'd have to make drastic changes in your life.

Be especially watchful of what you are conveying about career choices in your life. If you constantly complain about what you do for a living, there may be messages that you are sending your children that they don't need.

- It's more important to earn lots of money than to enjoy what you do for the majority of each day.
- Money is a burden in life, not a tool.
- What anyone does all day to earn money is a necessary evil.

If your child learns these unspoken messages from you, she's less likely to want to take control of her own money or begin to earn it herself. After all, if money is painful to acquire, she'd rather you just keep earning the money and getting her what she wants. If budgeting it is a sacrifice, she'll let you worry about that and she'll just let you know what you need to buy her. If you are in an unhappy career situation, explore your own alternatives. Doing so may be one of the best lessons you can teach your child. It will show that there can be a balance between having the money you need and being happy. It can also show her that it's okay to explore changes. She's not stuck with her first career choice. It may not be easy, but you and your family will be happier for it.

Checking Accounts

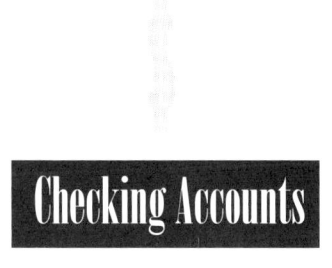

"How pleasant it is to have money!"
-Arthur Hugh Clough

Bank accounts are a convenient, safe place to keep money. They can also be instrumental in a couple of financial lessons. One is the concept that money can make money when saved properly. This is part of what is covered in the chapter on Savings.

The other concept is how to use a checking account. For most kids a checking account becomes practical about the time they start a job, start buying their own clothes, or start driving. For some, this is all around the same time. They can use the checking account to pay for regular purchases and the first few bills they may have.

Most banks have their own requirements for minors who have a bank account that incorporate local, state, and federal requirements as well as their own internal policies. You may want to check out any requirements in your area (your banker can probably answer your questions) or you might want this to be an issue your child explores. This may be one of the times when you give them information it might normally take them awhile to find on their own, just to give them the opportunity to learn from you and realize that you're a great resource. For instance, you can tell your child that she might be able to get checks cheaper from a discount mail service. Ultimately, though, she either uses that information to her benefit and realizes you're pretty smart, or she doesn't.

Before you allow one of your children to open a checking account, make sure she has been told how an account works. You can show her how to keep a running balance in her check register. Often a better first step is to go to a friendly bank and have the new accounts representative explain the bank's schedule of regular charges, including charges for insufficient funds. After this, you can inform your child of the consequences of an overdraft from your perspective. You may decide that an overdraft will result in closing the account. You might feel that having to pay the charges involved with an overdraft would be an appropriate consequence. Another condition of opening a checking account could be that your child shows you the account reconciliation each month for some time period—like six months. After that, she's on her own. Lastly, you may want to require some basic training on such items as how to fill out a check and how to fill out deposit slips. That instruction can come from you, from the banker, or from some other research that your child does.

This is a great opportunity to require some inexpensive research of services in general. There are neighborhood banks, online banks, and credit unions to choose from. Ideally your child does the research and finds out which is best for her situation. You can give her a basic list of items to research. For instance:

- Is there a monthly service charge? If so, how much?

- If the account has a check presented for payment and there isn't enough money to cover it, what is your procedure?
- Are my canceled checks returned with my statement?
- How do I order checks? What's the cost of checks?
- Do you waive any of your service charges or minimum balance requirements for minors?
- Is there a minimum amount needed to open an account?
- What do I have to present to the bank to open an account? This might be forms of identification, a birth certificate, etc.
- Are there other benefits or services that come to a particular bank's checking account customers?

Be sure that you are aware of the consequences for your child as well as the consequences for you of having her open her own bank account. She may decide that the bank across town has the best deal for her. That's fine as long as she doesn't expect you to drive her there every time she wants to make a deposit or a withdrawal. If she has an overdraft in her account—even if it's from an innocent mathematical error—it might end up on a credit report for her. To start off a credit history with a negative report can be quite a financial handicap. Your bank might require a joint owner on the account, in which case an overdraft might also end up on your credit report. One alternative is to put a small cushion of money that is your money into the account. Each month you review the bank statement and if the balance has dipped into your cushion, she owes you an overdraft fee. You could do the same thing with an overdraft protection line that's provided by the bank. If she goes into it, she has to pay you an overdraft fee.

If your child is chronically out of money for the things she truly needs such as clothes or lunch money, she might not be ready for a checking account. In this case, you can set some goals with her for being able to open a checking account. For instance, you could say that once she has saved up $200, you'll take her to open a checking account.

The advantage to your child of having a checking account is that it's a safe, convenient way to pay for items and keep track of how much money is being spent as well as how much money she has. Also, your child might find some conveniences that you're not familiar with. For instance, one parent said her son opted not to have checks and only use a debit card. As long as he's checking his balance and keeping track of his purchases, this can be very efficient. The same can be said for having recurring payments automatically taken from a checking account. As long as the money's always there, it helps ensure a good credit rating and bills that are up-to-date.

Credit Cards

"Pay every debt, as if God wrote the bill."
-Ralph Waldo Emerson

Credit cards have become a financial plague for many adults. People are spending more than they make and the interest charges will ensure that they will have heavy debt payments for years to come. Used properly, however, credit cards can be a lifesaver in a financial emergency, serve as a financial organizational tool, and be a convenient way to consolidate and simplify your personal finances. To the extent that kids become exposed to charge cards, they need to start learning it all—the good, the bad, and the ugly.

Many financial professionals would make a distinction between a credit card and a charge card. A charge card is one that must be paid in full when each bill is received. A credit card may be paid when the bill comes in or the balance can be paid over several months. The terms are used interchangeably here.

Having a credit card that your child can use in an emergency could literally be a lifesaver. About the time he and his friends start to drive, they'll have more outings where they are out unsupervised. It's actually a good idea for the sake of safety to have a credit card your child can use if he ever goes out of town without you. At that point you can either apply for a credit card in his name or get a card on your account that allows him to sign for purchases. If you use this method and you aren't yet comfortable with his ability to make decisions that you're willing to pay for, you should keep the card and only give it to him in situations where he'd be allowed to use it in case of an emergency, such as when he's on an out-of-town sports team trip. If you get him a card in his name, you can pretty much count on having to be a co-signer or guarantor. In either case, tell him up front what you consider an acceptable emergency for which the card can be used. This may be a flat tire or a taxi ride home from a party if his ride has left him or has been drinking. Also give some examples of unacceptable "emergencies" such as a CD of his favorite group that was on sale or a pizza when he was really hungry. Outline what the result of using the card for a non-emergency would be. It should include some consequence in addition to paying for the charge on the card. One logical consequence would be to pay "interest" on the unacceptable purchase. Since financial transactions between parents and their minor children are not generally subject to usury limitations, it makes sense to have the surcharge be an amount that will really make an impression like 20% or 25% or a flat fee of $25 or $50 in addition to the cost of the non-emergency item.

Once your child has shown responsibility with emergency use of a credit card, you can let him start using the card for convenience. He can charge up to the amount of his monthly allowance in a month. When the bill comes in, though, he must pay for his purchases in full. If he can't pay for them in full, charge him the highest rate allowed in your state, whether that's the rate on the card or not. Require him to pay a substantial share of the discretionary portion of his allowance toward the card charges until they're paid. If he gets behind or takes more than three or four months to pay off credit card charges, "garnish" his allowance.

If he gets so far in debt with the card that he's going to need more than six months to pay it back, you may need to take the card away until it's paid. If the card needs to be taken away, consider restricting his activities to ones where he couldn't possibly have a financial emergency. This could have a limiting effect on his activities. If that scenario develops, make sure that you phrase the restriction in a way that shows that it's a consequence, not an arbitrary punishment. For instance, instead of saying, "You're grounded until this is paid!", you could say, "Just so you can plan accordingly, you won't be able to have any out-of-town outings until this is paid. Obviously you can't use the credit card, and I'm just not comfortable if you're out somewhere that you might have a financial emergency without the credit card." The result is the same for your child, but it has put the consequence squarely in his court and shown that you care about his well-being.

To recap, credit cards can be a great convenience and part of a financially responsible life. If misused, they can lead to disaster. For your kids to learn responsible use of credit cards while they're young can help avoid problems when they're on their own.

Personal Notes

Debt Used Wisely

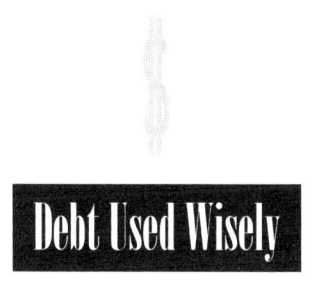

"There can be no freedom or beauty about a home life that depends on borrowing and debt."
- Henrik Ibsen

Most financial planners will tell you there's good debt and bad debt. The best kind of good debt gives you a tax break for borrowing money to do something that society thinks is a good idea. The most common example is buying a house. There are also breaks for borrowing money for higher education (student loans). Also, an acceptable use of debt might be to buy a car. If you need a car to get a better job and you don't happen to have the cost of a car in savings, a car loan could be good debt, even though you don't get tax breaks for the interest. If you buy a car worth four times your annual income to impress potential dates, that car loan is probably a bad kind of debt. Credit cards (unless paid off each month) are usually examples of very bad debt. As too many adults have experienced, if credit cards go on in a chronic state of carrying balances, the interest charges—which over time can amount to more than was originally charged—will cause the debt for short term items like meals and vacations to take years to pay.

Children can start getting the concept of debt very young. Within a year or two of your child receiving an allowance, she can be introduced to using debt. In all likelihood, it's not a concept you need to introduce—she will do it. At some point she'll want to buy something she doesn't have enough money for and she'll ask if she can borrow some money from you. There may be some reasons that you'd see as legitimate for this—like the item being on sale or supplies may run out—and some that you don't—"I want it now." There is a fine line for you as a parent between controlling how she spends her money and being a wise lender. This is a reality of our adult financial lives, though. You might not be able to get a loan for a vacation from your conservative neighborhood bank, but there probably is a lender who'll make that loan and charge you nosebleed interest rates for the privilege of borrowing.

First of all, have her think through why she believes waiting isn't a good option. Also, the purchase should be something that will last longer than it takes her to pay you back. For instance, you probably wouldn't want to lend her money for a dessert, but you might be willing to lend her money for a CD. Once you and she agree that borrowing may be okay, you can go to the next step, which is determining how much to borrow. It's a good idea for you to know ahead of time what your own rules are in this regard. Up through elementary school, I suggest never lending more than half of a purchase price. Also, the loan should be an amount that can be repaid in no more than a month. So if your daughter wants to buy a doll that costs $10 and she only has $1, no loan. If she has $6, you can loan her the other $4. If she wants a portable stereo that costs $100, she has $60, and her allowance is only $5 a week—that would stretch the loan out too long for someone her age. If, however, she can tell you how she'll augment her allowance (sweeping driveways for neighbors for a fee, household chores that you'd be willing to pay for, etc.) then you might be willing to make that loan. She has to stay on schedule for paying the loan back in a reasonable time.

When your child gets into middle school or junior high, she should also start paying interest. She has been exposed through school to the mathematical concepts she needs to understand the idea. You don't necessarily have to use market interest rates. It may be best to use a simple monthly charge. For instance, if she borrows $30, every week she needs to understand that $1 of every weekly payment goes to use as a finance charge. By the end of high school, she needs to be charged regular interest, just like she would be at a bank.

There are a couple of very important concepts your child needs to be exposed to throughout the debt learning process. The first is repossession. When you loan her money, you've established up front what her minimum payments are. If she gets more than one payment behind, the item she used the loan to buy needs to be repossessed. I don't mean that you take the item until she's caught up on payments, I mean you repossess it and keep it, just like a bank would. This may seem harsh, but it's much better to have your pre-teen lose a stereo to you than to have her lose a car to the repo man for late payments. It doesn't matter if you want what she bought or not—especially the first time you have to repossess. After all, banks end up with all kinds of junk. The second concept is that of a credit history. If she gets behind on a payment, don't lend her money the next time she asks. The next time after that, you might lend her the money, but require her to save up more of the down payment and charge her more interest. Make sure you explain these consequences. "I'll lend you the money, but I don't want what you're buying. I just want my money back. Based on how you paid me back before, I won't loan you the money unless you have 75% of the cost saved up and I want $1.50 in interest each week." Like any consumer, she can either take the terms offered, find another source for the money, or do without the purchase.

Remember that a basic tenet of debt is that you shouldn't take longer to pay for something than its useful life. For instance, you don't want a 20-year car loan, but you could probably feel comfortable with a 20-year home loan. Any time that your child wants to borrow money for something, stick to this rule of thumb in deciding if you'll lend the money. If you waiver from the rule, she loses interest in making the payments and repossessions can lose their impact.

If your child did well with her borrowing in the past, she may be ready for her first real loan in high school. Most kids shouldn't be borrowing money until they can have a steady job, even if it's a part-time one. You may have the dilemma of not wanting to buy your child her first car, but still wanting her to have her own vehicle in high school. If she has to get a job to pay the loan, it could affect her grades and ability to engage in extracurricular activities that will greatly enhance her ability to be self-sufficient in the future. Having your child be financially responsible shouldn't mean that she gets into a mentality that she has to work all the time to have her basic needs met. Most kids should be responsible for paying for their own car insurance and that can usually be accomplished from a summer job if the money is saved and budgeted properly. When she's going to be responsible for all or part of the cost of a vehicle, it's a good first bank loan to deal with. This can also be a time to get her motivation behind researching a major purchase. You may need to co-sign or guarantee a loan through a public lending institution and you should take it as seriously as you would getting a loan in your own name. If she doesn't pay in a timely manner, it will probably have an effect on your credit rating as well as hers. If the loan is primarily in her name, it will be the first step toward establishing a credit history for her. How she handles it will determine whether or not she has to deal with cleaning up her credit or having a good credit history established early in life.

During the end of high school, if she will need any student loans to go to college or trade school, researching the available loans should be her responsibility to the extent possible. You will have to provide your personal financial information unless she qualifies as independent for loan purposes. It may be helpful to review what she's doing and give her some guidance, but leaving the final responsibility to her has a couple of positive consequences. One is that she understands that the loans will ultimately be her responsibility and she is aware of what the terms of the loans are. Secondly, she may be more motivated in her education to do well since she knows she's paying for it.

If it has been pretty smooth sailing for her in establishing credit and paying according to loan terms, she may get a credit card offer in her name even before she graduates from college. If she qualifies for a card, she may have already developed a good payment ethic. If she gets in over her head, don't give her the money to pay it off. This may be one of the toughest decisions you ever make. You can offer tips or tell how you've managed to pay off difficult debts in the past, but your actions will speak much louder than any words you can muster. If you pay the card for her, she'll learn—consciously or unconsciously—that any time she gets in over her head, it will miraculously work out without any pain or sacrifice on her part.

Once she has some credit in her name, have her get a copy of her credit report, which she can do by contacting the credit reporting agency and request a copy. If she hesitates, you might need to make it a condition for something you are doing for her. You can go over it with her, but it might be even better to ask a loan officer at your bank to explain the report to her. Besides showing her what the overall score suggests, they can usually tell items that will reflect well (like making payments on time) and items that will reflect poorly (like too much in credit card debt). Most of these items on a credit report reflect positively or negatively for a reason, and hearing from a professional what the effect is can often help to establish good habits early.

Discretion

"Small pitchers have wide ears."
- John Heywood

Too many people go to unhealthy extremes in their candor or lack thereof when it comes to finances. In some families, parents flash their money around, brag about how much they make, and give minute detail of what they pay for luxuries to anyone who will listen. At the other extreme, many families never discuss any financial issues. In these families, money—like sex—is a taboo subject that is not brought up by parents and is squelched in conversation if it does come up.

Some financial issues are a matter of public record. If you wonder what your friend the teacher makes, you can call the school district and find out the range of salaries for teachers with his experience. If you want to know the compensation of the president of a publicly traded company, it's laid out pretty explicitly in the company's securities filings. If you wonder what your neighbor who is self-employed makes, there's probably not an easy way to get that information without asking him—and it's probably none of your business.

And that's where kids need to begin understanding about what to tell and what not to tell about finances. There are some items that are not anyone else's business and they need to keep those items to themselves. Within the relationship they have with you, however, they should feel free to discuss anything about their money, and candor about your own money lays the best foundation for this. Your actions will teach more on this issue than your words. When it comes to your first dealings with your child about money, be straightforward. You might even want to be a little formal. Let's say that you're going to talk to your son about establishing an allowance. Ask him to sit down with you at the kitchen table. Make sure he's paying attention. Tell him that you want to start paying him a little money every week, what he has to do to receive it, and what he should expect to spend it on. It's really important that you ask him if he has any questions. It's just as important that you tell him before you finish the conversation that if he has any questions about his allowance in the future, just ask you. He has the ability to ask you a question or seek your advice rather than make a mistake, so tell him that. That being said, he'll make some mistakes and learn from them and you will need to be as communicative with him as possible when that happens. If money has been a taboo subject in your house and he believes he's just supposed to intuitively know everything he needs to know about it, he's not going to want to ask questions or discuss his mistakes with you.

It's just as difficult to establish what it's not okay to talk about outside of the family. For most kids, the best way to keep a secret is to have someone they can tell. That's you! As you're discussing career options with your child, you might want to tell him your earnings history—what you made in your first job, how much of a raise you got with your first big promotion, and what you make now. You should tell him up front that you don't want people outside the family to know about it, but that he can discuss it with you and your spouse any time he thinks it would be helpful. Whenever he gets a piece of financial information about the family, you should tell him if you don't want it discussed with anyone else.

For example, if you tell your child how much money you earn, you will probably tell him not to discuss that. You can explain that, although they shouldn't, some people judge a person by how much or how little he makes. Also, there are those who will try to manipulate or take advantage of another's finances if they can. Being discreet about income helps to minimize these situations. Also, some of us just don't want the world knowing what we earn any more than we want to announce how much we weigh. It's just a courtesy to honor another's desire for privacy, and a privilege to be included in that information.

Also, there may be some assumed differences in financial situations, but discussing them is offensive or embarrassing to those involved. If your child's friend lives in a house that's much smaller than yours, discussing what your house cost might embarrass the friend. It might also be perceived as bragging. Again, it often comes down to courtesy and consideration of another's feelings, as well as keeping money from being some type of value gauge.

What happens when there is an indiscretion with financial information? The consequence of each mistake your child makes should be a logical one. When word gets out that someone can't keep a secret, they don't get told any more secrets. And as a parent, you'll want to let him know that. Ultimately he'll either prove that he can be trusted to be discreet or he won't have access to any more private information.

Personal Notes

Divorce, Kids, and Money

"A torn jacket is soon mended, but hard words bruise the heart of a child."
-Henry Wadsworth Longfellow

This topic can be emotionally devastating to everyone it touches. There are enough issues to fill several books. Some basic principles need to be followed by parents who go through a divorce.

Don't use your children or money as a weapon to harm your former spouse. "We can't have your birthday party because your dad doesn't pay enough." "I'd love to take you on vacation, but we can't afford to. Your mom got all my money!" Be honest with yourself. These aren't financial issues, they're emotional ones. When parents divorce, the healthiest emotional situation for the child is to get full emotional support from both parents. Saying or doing things that make the child feel that she has to choose between her parents is unfair and often emotionally devastating. Don't do it.

Don't talk to your child about financial disagreements with your ex-spouse. Don't even talk about these disagreements within earshot of your child. It doesn't matter if you are the spouse who is getting money or if you are the spouse who might have to pay money. Don't drag your child into that argument.

Make your child support and alimony payments on time. If there are legitimate circumstances that necessitate a change in these financial obligations, discuss them privately with your ex and have them changed through the legal system. Otherwise, honor these obligations. Any household where your child spends time needs to have a lifestyle that you want him to have. Many parents say, "I'll pay child support, but I don't want to pay anything that goes toward my ex's lifestyle!" Let's face it. Your ex isn't going to stay in a tent while your child has the use of the house. When they share a home, it's the same home for both of them. In many divorces, if there is a reasonably fair financial settlement, both parents have to tighten their belts afterwards. Also, both are often going to spend less time with the children than they did when the family was together. Accept that and move forward from it.

But most of all, don't put the kids in the middle.

Earning Money

"The first consideration for all, throughout life, is the earning of a living."
- Jean Racine

Children in elementary school are usually able to start earning money in addition to their allowance. It's a good idea to give them six months to a year to see how they do with their allowance. During that period when they're introduced to the concept of having their own money, be aware of what lessons they're learning. They may be able to do some extra chores around the house and get paid for them. The pay should be based on at least two criteria: it should be something that you'd pay someone else to do, and children should get paid in accordance with their skills. For instance, if your shoes need to be sorted and put away in your closet, don't pay your son to do it if you wouldn't pay someone else to do it. If you would pay someone to take care of your lawn, but you know you're going to have to help your child because he can't do it on his own yet, don't pay him what you'd pay an outside service.

I remember when I was young having a "work day" for a group I was in. Each of us kids was supposed to do something to bring a certain amount of money to the group treasury on a predetermined Saturday. My fellow group members were doing recycling gathering, having bake sales, and sweeping driveways. I had a few little projects that I was participating in and my mom told me that she needed a manicure and told me what she'd pay me for it. I'd never done a manicure, but I'd seen them done and it looked like easy money to me. About half way into the manicure my mom said, "You're not doing a very good job. I don't want to pay for this if you're not going to do any better than this." It had the desired effect. In this case, I'd taken on something I couldn't do well. She and I agreed on a lower price, I did the best I could, and I had to find another project to make the rest of my share of the money my group needed.

The concept your child needs to get is that he can get money for doing things that people are willing to pay him to do. And he can spend that money on things he wants or needs. My kids tuned in to that very quickly after each of them was introduced to the idea. Because my husband and I are both self-employed, we allowed our kids to do little office jobs for us for minimum wage around the time they each got into second grade. That's a young age to introduce someone to the work force, but we limited their work time to an hour or so at a time. Each child made minimum wage and their work was usually something like shredding or punching holes in the pending filing. Everything they did was something that I would have to pay someone to do. Often one of our daughters would offer to do something like polish all the furniture. If it didn't need polishing, she had a choice. She could polish furniture and not get paid for it or she could do some of the work that we would pay for.

Some very interesting thinking was soon visible in each of our children when they started working. The amount of money they got for working one hour was almost exactly what we paid each of them in weekly allowance at the time. So any time there was an item one of them was saving for, they would talk through with their dad or me how many weeks they'd have to save or how many hours they'd have to work to buy the desired item. The next mental step each one of them took was that when there was work that I'd offer to them, they'd be more likely to take it even if they didn't have a shopping wish list. They were learning that if you save money when you have the opportunity, you don't have to work for or borrow the money when something comes along that you need.

When your child gets old enough to have a job with regular hours and pay, you need to establish some acceptable parameters. After all, you don't want your 16-year-old to have a great high-school career in fast food while flunking his sophomore English class. Establish expectations up front and stick to them. Some good starting points for these rules are maintaining a specific grade point average, getting a reasonable amount of sleep, and not imposing on the rest of the family without permission. For instance, if your 15-year-old wants to work at a gas station five miles away, should he assume that you'll drive him to and from work without discussing it with you? Even if you agree to do this, you might want to have him pay something for gas or your time. There are consequences for taking on obligations that involve other people and your kids need to learn that. Also, some jobs just aren't worth taking. It may be because they are inconvenient—across town, lousy hours, pay is too low. It may be because the work isn't interesting. Ironically, that can be some of the long-term value for the child. Rather than you telling him why he needs to get an education and learn a skill, he learns firsthand why he doesn't want to do the only jobs he's qualified for without an education.

For you to begin discussing these issues with your child at an early age opens the door for a lifetime of being a resource to him. He's much more likely to call you when he's got an opportunity to change jobs in his late twenties if he was able to discuss his first few jobs in high school with you. He's also more likely to make valid career decisions if he's learned about working early on.

This is one of the many areas where you teach by your actions as well as your words. If you are constantly complaining about your work, your boss, and what you do all day, your kids are learning that work is a necessary evil and something they'd rather avoid. If you come home from work happy, share good stories about your workplace, and take your child with you to work for a visit, he doesn't feel negative about work. He also feels that it's a part of your life that he's included in.

My youngest asked to go to the office with me on a day when the kids didn't have school. I think she was in the third grade at the time. It was a day when I'd only be working half a day so I told her she could go with me, but that she'd need to get up and be ready to go at the time I normally went to the office. She was ready on time and she was really ready. Since the kids worked in a supply room that clients don't see or on weekends when we're closed to the public, I didn't usually have them dress up when they went to my office. My daughter, however, had on one of her nicest dresses. It was a white dress with a pleated skirt. The sleeves and the skirt had navy blue trim around them. To really dress up, she was wearing hose. The hose were red, but I still realized that she had seen how I dressed to go to work and decided that she needed to look really nice if she was going to go to work on a real work day. When we headed home after a few hours, I paid her the hourly wage she earned plus I paid her a little bonus. I explained to her that a bonus is something that is an unexpected payment for work that was beyond what you had to do and that her attention to her professional outfit was appreciated. I further explained that while bonuses are great, she should always just do her best, not try to shoot for bonuses. She learned about the value of professionalism and she let her brother and sister know all about it when we got home.

There are a couple of valid ways to look at when to start kids in the life of earning income. One is that they can be exposed to earning money at a young age and see that it can be enjoyable. Another is to say that they'll have the rest of their life to earn money and they don't need to lose their childhood by working. Pushing them to earn money too young or allowing them to graduate from high school without any sense of earning money are both extremes you don't want to go to. If you feel that earning money is a horrible thing that should be avoided as long as possible, you may want to rethink your own career and your own attitudes about earning money. If you think the only thing worth doing is working nonstop, that's worth rethinking, too.

A Bright Leitz Money Map Book

Personal Notes

Education Funding

> "The direction in which education starts a man will determine his future life."
> - Plato

There is a common misconception among much of the middle class that failure to pay for a child's college education is a form of child abuse. This is not the case. In fact, many people who pay partially or completely for their own education gain a great sense of accomplishment in doing so. Some of these people have even said that they feel that being financially responsible for their college education has given them a greater sense of appreciation for it than if someone else—like their parents—had paid for it. One thing is certain. If you sacrifice your own financial well-being to send your kids to college, no one is better off. When these children become well-educated adults they then feel morally obligated to support their parents. They may even do this to their own financial detriment. So sending your kids to college at all costs—literally—doesn't do them any favors.

A key to education funding is setting expectations. Starting in grade school you can (and should) encourage your child to get an education that will allow her as many alternatives to enjoy life—financially and otherwise—as possible. By middle school she should understand that higher education isn't free and you should start talking about how she can expect such an education to be paid for. If you have the ability to pay for college and can do so, you can put that out as a possibility. It's a good idea not to promise too much. So many things—divorce, a poor economy, losing a job, family illness, poor investment choices—can impact your ability to write a check for college. It's best to leave the possibility on the table that she may need to get student loans, work part-time, or have a work-study program as well as encouraging her to be willing to explore scholarships and grants.

Once a child is starting high school, you can start being more specific about the costs of college and exploring the possible schools and financial alternatives that might be available to her. This should be as much a part of the discussion as what to choose as a major, where to live, and campus safety.

A college education isn't right for everyone. Too many young people go to college because they aren't given any choice in the matter. They graduate with a degree they don't want and start a career they hate. Or they flounder through college with bad grades and no sense of direction or accomplishment. All that being said, college can be a great place for young people to explore areas of potential interest and find their passion. If they are forced to pursue a degree and not given much choice in what they study, it may be more of a hindrance than a help. This is explored more in the chapter on Careers. Any education dollars, whether they are spent by you or your child, will have a greater return if the education gives her a way to earn a living doing something she loves.

Future Goals

"We should all be concerned about the future because we will have to spend the rest of our lives there."
-Charles Franklin Kettering

Many people live "hand to mouth" virtually all of their lives. When money comes in, it goes straight back out and there's nothing much to show for it. For far too many, it's a formula with an even more negative outcome. They know that money is coming, so they commit to something with that money. The money is literally gone before they get it. Your child can learn to put something aside for future goals. This is slightly different than what is discussed in the chapter on Savings. Here we're looking at a specific goal for which money is earmarked as it's accumulated.

Generally children up to about the age of 10 have trouble saving for a goal that takes more than a month. Children up to their very early teens can usually save for a couple of months. In high school, a child who has been saving for future goals since she was young can probably have some very long-term goals that take several months or even years, such as a car or college.

This learning process can start relatively young on a small scale. Let's say your 7-year-old wants a toy that costs $18. She has $6 now and she makes $7 per week in allowance. Assuming this is a toy you don't expect to be sold-out in the next few weeks, this is an excellent first lesson in saving for a goal. It's also a good opportunity for her to use her math skills. Sit down with her with a sheet of paper in front of you where you can add up how long it will take her to save up for the toy. There's a form in the Appendix that you can copy for this purpose. Now she has $6. In a week she'll have $13. In another week she'll have $20, which can pay for the toy. I'd highly recommend that you make a calculation of the sales tax in your area and have her save enough to cover the entire purchase. This is a very minor amount, but if she doesn't pay for the whole purchase, she may get the idea that she pays for the big costs, but you always pick up the minor costs. Your next step is to discuss with her where she'd like to keep the money she's saving for the toy. If you want, you can offer to keep it for her. The advantage to this is that you can discuss it with her easily if she wants to spend the money on something else prior to meeting her goal. The disadvantage is that she might not feel in control of the money or her decision if she doesn't actually hold on to the cash herself. Each time she gets her allowance, it can be a good support to the process if you go with her to put the money in the place she's chosen to keep it and give her reinforcement on getting closer to the goal. "One more week and you can buy your toy!" When you're within a day or so of her having enough money for the much-anticipated purchase, set a time with her to go to the store for the toy. On that day, have her hold the money when you go to the store, give the money to the person at the register, and take the change. This may be a favorite toy for a long time because she made the effort to save for it.

The biggie for most young people is their first car. You need to think through your own tolerance level on what latitude you'll allow your child once he gets a car. It may teach a very wrong lesson to tell him that he must earn all the money for his first car and his own auto insurance and maintenance costs, but limit what type of car he can get and what he can use it for. Chances are above average that he'll raise the subject, but if he doesn't, it would be a good idea to address it with him about six months before he gets his learner's permit. Let him know what financial commitment he will have, whether that's paying for the entire car, paying for regular maintenance, paying for fuel and insurance, or some combination of these factors. If he might need a loan for the car, have him do some research about what's involved. If you need to cosign or have the loan in your name (which you probably will, since he's a minor), discuss what you'd require to commit yourself on the loan and what the consequences are if a problem arises with it. It might have the effect that he'll start saving for a down payment and other potential expenses. It might also have the effect of having him get serious about earning money. This is addressed in the Vehicles chapter, too.

Ultimately, a great outcome in regard to teaching your child to save for future goals is that he thinks ahead about what he wants, calculates what he needs to save and for how long, works toward the goal, and has the satisfaction of reaching it. Long-term, that can translate into an adult who saves up for a first home, retirement, and other goals he cares about. As always, sometimes the failures are as valuable as the triumphs. Having to bum rides off friends and family members because he didn't make the effort to save for a car is probably more effective than you dragging him through the process of saving.

Personal Notes

Gifts

"I notice this each year I live:
I always like the gifts I get,
But how I love the gifts I give!"
-Carolyn Wells

There are several categories of gifts that can be learning opportunities for your kids. There are the monetary gifts they receive, the gifts they give their friends, and the gifts they give to family.

Most kids get money from family periodically. Decide up front how you expect the gift to be treated. Before your child is in school, it's best to make the decision without input from her. If you put that money into savings, it's fine to tell her that. You can even say what the savings are for, like college. About the time that she's in grade school, it's a good idea to show her the bank statements for the savings after she gets a gift. That's another opportunity to talk about the goal that the savings are for. Having the gifts diverted to a savings account can work well all the way through high school for many families. If your child is making wise decisions with her money in high school, you can start letting her make the decision about what to do with monetary gifts.

If you pay for gifts that your child gives to friends for birthdays and other occasions, it's always a good idea to set a budget. You might have the same budget for all friends or you might have a slightly larger budget for close friends. Either way, the child needs to make choices that fit into the budget. At 10, my youngest daughter had great fun doing a hodgepodge of different small items for friends. When she had hit the limit of what we'd pay for the gift, she decided the gift was complete. She had fun picking out the items and the recipient and the others at the party thought it was a fun idea, too. It's important to avoid having the child get into the habit of trying to match a gift she receives in terms of price. Families need to do what they think works given their own income and what they think it's appropriate to give. It's never too early to have your kids learn that "keeping up with the Joneses" is unnecessary.

Giving to others—especially family members that might tend to be taken for granted—is a good way for kids to keep things in perspective. As long as you are paying, you need to establish a budget for each gift. You will probably also want to make sure that the child's list of gift recipients is complete. This is another time when the child has a chance to exercise her own choices in what to buy. If something is truly inappropriate, you might step in and exercise your right to refuse to pay for something and give some good alternative suggestions. When kids are in preschool and early elementary grades, it's good to pick a very modest budget for a gift for each person the child should give to at holidays or on birthdays. When our kids were very small, every Christmas my husband and I would both take them to a store where everything cost a dollar or less. We both went so that we could help the children at the checkout counter with the other parent's gift. We have some great family memories from these early learning experiences. I was totally baffled why our older daughter bought her three-year-old sister a spatula. I quizzed her a little while she was wrapping it and she explained that it was for the sand box. Sure enough, it was a big hit and the recipient knew exactly what it was for. I certainly wouldn't have thought of that as a gift choice. The same daughter one year bought a night-light that was a six-inch-high white Virgin Mary as a gift for her father. She was simply overwhelmed by the beauty of it. I suppose we love religious symbols as much as any family, but this thing was really gaudy. Without telling my husband what the gift was, I had to warn him — and all the other adults in the family — not to laugh when he opened it. Everyone reacted with the proper amount of awe when it was opened and the giver was very pleased.

As kids reach an age where they are earning their own money, you may decide to have them include the gifts they give in their budget. Given that most children don't earn enough to meet all their financial needs until they get their first full-time job, it's reasonable to give them a gift budget each year until they are fully employed. You might also find that as your children get older, they supplement the budget you give them for gifts. This is a good example of the child making his own decisions about what he'll do with his money. Even if you disagree with the allocation of funds, it's his money and he'll deal with the consequences.

A Bright Leitz Money Map Book

Personal Notes

Grandparents

"Because they are usually free to love and guide and befriend the young without having to take daily responsibility for them, they can often reach out past pride and fear of failure and close the space between generations."
- Jimmy Carter
U.S. Presidential Proclamation of National Grandparents' Day

We've probably all heard someone say something to the effect that grandkids are the best reason to have kids. Grandparents come in a variety of temperaments. Some feel that it's their God-given right to spoil their grandkids. These grandparents let their grandkids have and do things their parents won't. Others feel that their grandkids are already spoiled rotten. And of course there are lots of varieties in between these extremes.

Ideally, your kids' grandparents will respect and support the lessons you are teaching your children. If so, you can communicate with them that you are trying to give your child the ability to make informed financial decisions and accept responsibility for the outcome of those decisions. That would mean that the grandparents can't bail the child out of poor decisions or buy his affection with money. That doesn't mean that they can never give money as a gift or reward. Give the grandparents a general overview of how the money relationship is developing with your child. Also, offer to be available to them for input on financial gifts and rewards that they want to give. They can also give verbal support for lessons that the children are learning. They can be a part of this learning environment for their grandchildren.

If you have some grandparents that are determined that it's their job to spoil their grandkids and keep them from ever wanting for anything or having an unhappy decision, you can deal with that too. Studies of children after a divorce have indicated that children deal better with different family structures than with conflict, so just enforce your philosophy when the children are with you and realize that they may be experiencing something different when they are with their grandparents. Children often get different signals from home, friends, media, and school. They will make their own decisions and this is another example.

A place where grandparents can offer huge help is sharing their experience. Kids, especially very young ones, are sometimes more likely to listen to grandparents than to parents. Encourage grandparents to share their own memories of money—what things cost when they were young, their first job, their first purchase of a house or car, a significant money struggle in their experience, mistakes they made with money, how they saved for their retirement. This doesn't need to be done in a preaching instructional tone. It can just be family members sharing their memories, which gives grandparents, parents, and children something money can't buy.

Investments

"Americans want action for their money. They are fascinated by its self-reproducing qualities if it's put to work."
- Paula Nelson

Just about everyone has played the game Monopoly. You know that every time you pass Go you get $200. Have you ever see someone win the game without buying any of the properties? Think of the $200 you get for passing Go as the money you get from a job or career. You can sometimes stay in the game with only the salary, but to really have a chance of winning, you have to invest some of what you make. This is a beginning concept of investing that can introduce kids to the idea of using their money to make money.

The next stage in understanding the concept is that true investing is long-term. It's not day trading or even buying Park Place and getting money the next time someone lands on it. It's putting money away and not touching it for a long time so it will help you—the investor—meet a goal. This is also different from simply saving. Investing involves putting money into some type of vehicle—the investment—that may have more risk than letting a bank or credit union hold onto the money until you ask for it.

One of the best ways to show people the concept of investing is with what investment professionals call a mountain chart. You can usually get these from your investment advisor or from some financial internet sites. It's a graph that shows the price of a given investment or index over some period of time. It gets its name from the fact that it looks like one side of a mountain with jagged peaks and troughs. A mountain chart for a stock or stock index will probably have some pretty big variations over a 10 or 20 year period. A mountain chart for inflation or government bonds, on the other hand, will probably look like a gravel road—much less bumpy. These charts will also often show how much an initial investment grew to over a period of time. If you show this to your child, as young as 9 or 10, you can point out that for a long period of time some of the more risky investments can turn a little money into a pretty nice sum. Also point out the short-term downturns. Your child needs to understand that if she truly invests money, she'll get some investment statements that show that she has less money than she used to. Unless her investment goal is just around the corner, this is not an indication that it's time to bail out. She can also see as she gets closer to the goal that she needs to move into more conservative (also sometimes known as boring) investments or into an account that's just for short-term savings.

A version of another chart that investment professionals find helpful is in the Appendix. It illustrates that if an individual starts saving $3,000 a year at age 22 and stops when she's 30, she actually can end of up with more than if she starts saving $3,000 a year at age 31 and quits when she's 60. The annual amount isn't all that important, although $3,000 bears a surprising resemblance to what lots of people put into an IRA each year, but the point is the value of starting to invest early in life and letting compounding do some of the work. In the Appendix, I've added a column to the usual chart and that third column shows what happens if the investor combines the two. She starts investing at 22 and doesn't stop until she's 60. Now that's some serious money!

Another way to show your child the value of investing is to show her an account that you have for some financial goal for her, like a college fund. When the statements arrive you can show her how much you've added since the last statement and how much the balance is up to. If she's impressed by the balance, you can explain that part of that is from what you contribute, but part of the balance is because the investment has earned money over the time you've been contributing to it.

When your child is in high school or on a semester break from college, she could take a class on investing. These are often offered by community colleges or investment firms. The classes aren't always very challenging academically, but offer a basic consumer approach to understanding investments. The instructors are sometimes investment advisors who teach the class in an effort to attract new clients. That doesn't mean that the information given out isn't valid, but you might want to review the outline for the course or talk to someone who's taken the class in the past before signing up. If you and your child take the class together, it could spark instructional discussions about money that you don't have to initiate.

A Bright Leitz Money Map Book

Personal Notes

Jobs

"The laborer is worthy of his reward."
- I Timothy

A way for your kids to feel that they have truly earned their own money is to get a job. Most kids won't get a first job outside the home until very late in middle school or once they get into high school. In all likelihood, a first job won't be prestigious or lead to a dream career. But it can give your child a taste of being in the work force—coming to work on time, being conscientious about duties, answering to a supervisor, getting a paycheck. For many, a job is the biggest step they take outside of their home or school to make them feel independent. There may be some unexpected opportunities for your child to get exposed to a "real" job outside the home. Perhaps neighbors ask if your child could pet-sit or pick up mail while they are on vacation or if he'd be willing to pick weeds for pay. Don't be too concerned about how young he is if the opportunity looks good and you have the ability to be flexible about it.

Because my husband and I are both self-employed, we've had our kids do jobs for us since they were all in elementary school. There was a day when the receptionist at our office had asked to have a vacation day because she had family in town. This employee virtually never takes vacation or sick leave, so we were glad to have her take a day off. It turns out that I had appointments back-to-back all day and I was going to be the only person in the office. I looked at who the clients were and realized that none of them would be concerned about the receptionist being gone, but I still didn't want them to walk into an empty reception area, so I asked my middle-school-aged daughter to come to the office with me that day. It was summer so she was out of school and she'd been asking to come to work at the office. Needless to say, I limited her duties quite a bit. All she was to do was to greet people as they entered, ask them if they'd like a beverage, get them a beverage, and come into my existing appointment and give me a note telling me that my next appointment had arrived. She was not to answer the phone and if anything else came up she could interrupt me to ask a question. The rest of the time she could read a book or play games on the computer. I guess all parents love those moments when seeing the world through their child's eyes gives something mundane new vitality and charm. She loved the entire day. She bustled in with the notes to announce each appointment with enthusiasm. All the beverages were beautifully presented and she made a list of all the drink choices that she let each client choose from. Signing for a package that was delivered was thrilling. Instead of playing computer games during her spare time, she wrote and bound an article about how wonderful it is to be a secretary, including a page thanking her parents, her siblings, and our vacationing receptionist for making it all possible. She had experienced the joy of being responsible and taking pride in doing a job well.

Getting paid was almost unnecessary, but it had a nice impact on the experience, too.

Remember that the choice of job is up to your child. She might not choose to do something that you find interesting, but it gives her a chance to explore things that might interest her and give a real-life taste of needing to show up for work regularly. There are some ground rules that are reasonable for you to set for your child's safety and your own convenience as well as enforcing family rules dealing with your morals.

- Transportation to and from her job has to be acceptable to you. She shouldn't expect you to drive across town so she can get to work. She also can't get rides with people you don't approve of. If she expects you to provide transportation to her job, she needs to clear the location and her schedule with you. You might even want to charge her for gasoline.
- You can restrict hours she works even if she's driving herself to and from work. If she's got a job where she has to walk to her car alone at 2:00 a.m. in a remote part of town, you can exercise a veto.
- She needs to learn and abide by responsible employee behavior. That includes being punctual, putting forth good effort, and giving proper notice when resigning from a job.
- There's a difference between her having to ask customers if they want fries with their order and having to wear a skimpy uniform. It might be that neither is your choice, but one of the two violates your morals and the other is just something that you wouldn't be willing to do.

As your child reaches her later years in high school and enters college, she might start looking for jobs that give her a taste of a future career. This can be very positive and an exciting and productive time for her in charting her future. Careers are discussed in the chapter by that name.

Living Expenses

"Treat people as if they were what they ought to be and you help them to become what they are capable of being."
– Johann W. Von Geothe

Just about everyone has had some unpleasant surprises during the time they began living on their own and paying their own expenses. Even if someone is pretty good about planning all the big expenses, there are hundreds of things that can come up for payment, many of which he has no control over. To try to make a list of all the possibilities would be futile. The list would seem infinite.

So how can you best prepare your child for making ends meet? One way is to let him have a look at how your family does it. There are several potential risks here. One is having your financial affairs become public knowledge. The Discretion chapter addresses some of the big issues here. Another is setting unrealistic lifestyle goals for your child. He will see what you spend and assume that he can spend the same amount. Combining the knowledge of living expenses with the reality of income from his own job will help balance his sense of reality in that regard. And don't hesitate to point out the discrepancies if you need to. Perhaps the most dangerous, though, is his potential judgment of the value of your choices. This could be the most painful for you. He may think you're hypocritical for telling him he needs to spend his money wisely on conservative purchases when you spend yours on a sports car. Or he may see the money you pay for vacations and dining out and ask why you're not putting that money toward his college education instead of expecting him to pay for it.

If you decide to let your child have exposure to real living expenses by way of knowledge of the financial realities of your household, there are several ways you could do it. One is to go over the expenses with him. If you use a computer program like Quicken or Money, print out some summaries showing expenses for several months in monthly increments. For instance, print out what was spent in December, January, and February, and look at them together in March. Also, you can print a summary for the last calendar year and calculate what the monthly average for each expense was for that year. This exercise will show that expenses don't always come in easy monthly nuggets that are easy to plan. The holidays are usually more expensive than usual in the gift and dining out categories. There may be an insurance premium that only comes quarterly or even annually. Vacations don't happen every month and they either get paid for in advance by saving for them or for several months after by paying off credit card balances. Either way, some of the things that your child probably takes for granted—food, housing, fuel for the car, entertainment—become line items. In the Appendix is a form that can be used for family living expenses. Quicken and similar computer programs also can produce a list of expenses on a monthly, quarterly, or annual basis.

The value of this reality check needs to be blended with what he can initially earn on his own. In all likelihood, he won't make as much in his first "real" job as you do now. At first, he won't be able to afford to buy his own home and take the kind of vacations that you do on what he'll be earning. If he's thinking that he won't need college or other specialized career training, this may be a good opportunity to revisit getting an education that will allow more earning power. Also, remember to bring in what you're saving for retirement. If he's reluctant to think about being tied to school or a job now, ask some questions that will help him think through having to work into his late sixties, his seventies, and beyond, to have the lifestyle that he has now. For instance, ask your child what he'd like to be doing when he's your age. Another method is to ask what he can do now. Find out the income for that job and, using a budget form like the one in the Appendix, take out the reasonable amounts for taxes, rent, utilities, food, insurance, phone…you get the idea. Keep the expenses reasonable for a person who's new to the workforce. Also compare those expenses to yours. Then have him think about what he'll have to live on when he retires, based on how much is left after all the expenses. If that doesn't make him think, just compare the expenses you and he discussed with your family's expenses and discuss the difference in lifestyle. Be careful not to overwhelm him. To a teenager making $7 an hour working on weekends, making ends meet can seem an insurmountable task. That can be a good opportunity to discuss why acquiring career skills is worthwhile.

One son in a family I know had little or no interest in college and he didn't seem to have a career plan other than that. After some coaching and support from his parents, they told him that at his age 18 he either had to start paying rent or move out if he wasn't in college. He found the idea of paying rent to his parents offensive, so he moved into a house with some friends. As some of his roommates moved out without notice or were late with their share of expenses, he tired of both his job—which didn't pay very well—and always having to remind others of their shared financial obligations. He's now in college.

The next level of involvement is only appropriate if your child shows the interest, but he can actually help write the checks that pay your monthly bills. He'll see that even though the bill was paid last month, it comes in again and has to be paid on a regular basis. He can even be involved in some of your decisions on regular bills. Should you pay the car insurance semi-annually to avoid the small charge for paying it monthly? If so, how does that affect the other bills that have to be paid and what's left for fun money?

No matter what you do, you may find yourself faced with a child who has ignored all of your instructional opportunities and who gets his own apartment, runs up bills that he can't pay, and asks to be bailed out of his self-inflicted misery. Don't jump in with the financial life preserver. Part of what everyone has to learn is dealing with the consequences of his actions. While offering to let him move back in with you may be a compassionate and reasonable thing to do, paying the existing bills isn't. He should have to deal with his creditors, even if it means incurring less than stellar credit ratings. And if he does move in with you, he needs to be ready to contribute toward the household finances. That includes something for his share of food, utilities, and rent. Becoming a monetary safety net can be harmful to his ability to becoming self-sufficient and it can become a financial black hole for you.

Pets

**"Animals are such agreeable friends—
they ask no questions, they pass no criticisms."
- George Elliot**

Have you ever had a "free" pet join the family? Maybe a family you know is moving and can't take the dog with them and you can have it and all the pet toys and food they have in return for giving it a good home. Or a cat shows up on your back steps on a cold day and you give it some milk and it just never leaves. By the time you get the legally required shots, buy food, and have an unexpected visit to the vet, your free pet has cost you several hundred dollars. And that's not taking into account any carpet stains from accidents or damage to your furniture. Most people are either Pet People or they're not. Pet People would say that you wouldn't get rid of a pet because of expense or inconvenience any more than you'd get rid of a child for the same reasons. Those who aren't Pet People would say, "What's the big deal? It's just an animal!" (My apologies to all you Pet People who either fainted or had your blood pressure shoot up. I'm a Pet Person, so I don't adhere to this attitude, but we all know it's out there.)

If your child wants a pet, she needs to be responsible for it and, if you want, that can include the financial responsibility. One basic way is that she can be responsible for the initial cost of the animal. You can include the initial supplies like cage, collar, vet bills, or whatever is needed. If she's old enough, have her call or go to stores to find out these costs. Make sure the list is complete and seems accurate. Once she's saved enough for the pet gear, you'll let her get the pet.

Another way that kids learn the financial responsibility of such a commitment is to know they'll be responsible for subsequent costs, some of which are unexpected. If the dog digs up your flowers, your child has to replace the flowers. If the cat tears up your sofa, the child has to pay for either a cover or part of the cost of a new sofa. During the times that this is most effective—usually prior to your child reaching high school age—you are actually in control in some way of the flow of her money. If most of her money comes through allowance, hand her the allowance and then have her hand back to you what she owes. If she needs to have a check from a job cashed, take her to the bank and have the share she owes handed over to you before leaving the building.

At the risk of belittling either kids or pets, there are many parallels in being financially responsible for them. If my child breaks something in a store, I can't generally say to the shopkeeper, "It was a kid that broke it, so the loss is your problem." The shopkeeper expects me to pay because society assumes that I'm responsible for the actions of my child. In like fashion, if an animal that is owned by a family (or a member of that family) ruins your neighbor's property, that person expects the owner to make good for the damages. If the owner is your child, she needs to step up for the costs. Sure, it might not be her fault, but it's not the neighbor's fault either and the animal doesn't have the financial resources to take care of it.

Personal Notes

Philanthropy

"Charity never faileth."
- I Corinthians

Most people who have a comfortable relationship with their finances give part of their money to charities. Your children can learn this from your example and from their own experience. In both cases, the lessons can be more powerful if you are pro-active about it.

When it comes to setting an example, you might be humble and quiet about your giving. That's appropriate, but your family needn't be kept in the dark about what you're doing. Even if you aren't comfortable with showing your kids your budget, you can let them know who the family gives to and why. For instance, if you attend a church or synagogue, let your kids know that you give to the church and what that money enables the church to do. Most churches don't get money from any source but contributions, some of which are in the form of bequests from estates, or from investment income from previous gifts. So just about everything from the light bill to the clergy salary comes from contributions. Maybe your family goes to the zoo and your kids really love the zebra so you contribute to the zoo every year. You can tell them how many days of food your contribution provides, or that the zoo couldn't afford to have people clean the zebra's cage if people who care about the zoo didn't contribute to it.

The most responsible approach for anyone in regard to charitable giving is to investigate the causes they feel strongly about and contribute to the charities that are truly meeting the needs of those causes. This research and thought process can be taught by allocating an amount of your charitable giving each year that you let your children be involved in. It doesn't need to be a big amount of money. Their job is to pick one or more organizations that they would like to see the money go to. They need to make a proposal to you as to why the money should go where they'd like it to go. You can ask them questions that they might have to research. Such as, how much of the organization's donations go to administrative overhead each year? Has management of the organization been accused of misusing funds and, if so, what was the outcome of the investigation of that matter? If the kids don't do the homework to answer your questions, no donation is made on their behalf.

You can also refuse to give to a cause that you don't want to support since it's actually your money. If you take that route, however, you need to give a complete explanation to the child who made the proposal. Let's say that you are strongly against animal testing and your child wants some of his money to go to an organization that uses animals for what you believe are unnecessary tests. You can ask all the research questions that bring up the issue and then tell him that you are not willing to support an organization that includes animal testing in its operations. The hardest part for you to say may be that when he is making his own decisions with where his charitable dollars go, he is welcome to consider that organization. We use this method with our kids and it's rewarding to see them thinking about needs other than their own. One daughter always includes the local animal shelter in her gifts. All the kids include some of the religious organizations that we are involved in.

Personal Notes

Rewards

"The reward of a thing well done, is to have done it."
- Ralph Waldo Emerson

Rewards are tricky. As parents we all want to reward what we think is right behavior—the things we'd like to see more. However, sometimes the things we'd like to encourage won't always have positive financial rewards. For instance, some parents or extended family give a child money for every A he gets in school. Most people would agree that good grades are a good thing. But will the child be rewarded financially as an adult for academic achievement? It depends. If he gets into a good college and pursues a major that will result in a financially lucrative career, the message regarding his choices makes sense. If, however, he gets good grades and decides to become a teacher or even a college professor, he's not as likely to be highly paid. That might not be right, but that's how our world works now.

Here's another example. You decide to give your child a monetary reward for keeping his room clean. Having a clean room (or as an adult having a clean house) has a great upside for most people. You can find things when you need them. The smell is usually better than a really messy living space. Friends are more likely to feel comfortable when they come over and you're less likely to be embarrassed. But does having a clean room make money? Usually not. And even professional maids and house cleaners don't get paid for cleaning their own houses.

Some rewards can be anticipated and some can't. If you're a bounty hunter, you know how much you get for bringing in each bad guy. If you work for pay, you're generally told up front how much you get paid and what is expected of you. Every once in a while, a bonus comes along. But generally, financial rewards can be anticipated. You can make your financial rewards work either on a completely predictable basis or not.

Here's another thing to remember with rewards. Be careful what you wish for. If you set up a reward for a behavior, you might get that behavior all the time and it might be something that you only wanted on an isolated basis. For instance, if you want your child to help you research your next vacation and reward him for doing so, how does he build on that? You're not going to have vacations every week and he's going to want a way to capitalize on that reward. Part of the message you send may be that rewards aren't always consistent and something that you can count on. That may be exactly the message that you think is realistic. But don't send a message that's demotivating. If you send a message that sometimes you have money and sometimes you don't and it's up to someone else which situation you're experiencing now, that's going to have your child feeling very negative about money and the control it has over his life.

Rewards can be tied to financial issues that might seem unrelated to your kids at first blush. Here's a strategy that can work if your kids are 10 or older. If your family spends too much eating out, have your kids take responsibility for helping you plan meals and making sure that dinners get started on time. Then give the kids 10% of what you've saved on dining out for the month. That sets realistic consequences and saves you money. If your kids grow up to think that all their food has to be purchased at a restaurant—even if it's fast food—it will cost them much more than if most of their food comes from their grocery budget and is prepared at home. This also saves you money.

A Bright Leitz Money Map Book

Personal Notes

Savings

"A penny saved is a penny earned."
- Benjamin Franklin

There are a couple of major forms of savings. One is for a specified long-term goal. That is addressed in the chapter Future Goals. The other is saving for unexpected expenses, which we'll talk about here.

As adults, we know that we need to keep money in savings "just in case". The unforeseen expense could be a car repair, an impromptu vacation, or being out of work. Formulas on what you should keep in savings for contingencies vary. Some financial planners recommend 10% to 20% of gross household income in savings. Others recommend that you keep three to six months of household expenses available. These are issues that kids will need to come to grips with as they become fully responsible for their own finances. But they need to be exposed to it early to start developing their saving muscles.

The conceptual introduction is much like that for saving for future goals. Your child might not have a goal in mind, but you can remind her of a time when she wanted something and had to wait to get it while she saved for it. There are a couple of ways to set up the savings and they can be used at the same time. One is to have one place where your child keeps her spending money and another where she keeps her savings. It can be two jars, one jar and one bank, a purse and a piggy bank—whatever makes sense for her and lets her still feel in control. The next step would be to discuss how much she's saving. If she takes a fourth of everything she gets and puts it in savings, she'll see the savings add up pretty quickly, but still have a good chunk of change that she can spend when she wants.

Another method is to put money in a bank account, probably a traditional savings account. Many banks or credit unions have policies that allow minors to have accounts without the minimum balance requirements. The process of having your child research a savings account is basically the same as that for researching a checking account, which is in the chapter Checking Accounts. She won't need to find out about the charge for checks, but she will need to investigate if there is a charge for having a small balance and if there is a limit on how many withdrawals she can make each month. Part of what you want to convey is that if money is saved, it can make some money while the financial institution is holding on to it. When interest rates are low, that's pretty hard to get excited about, but it's still a better return than keeping money in a can in her room or spending it.

My son actually brought up the idea of having a savings account before I introduced it. He was about 10 and said he wanted to put some money in the bank. I asked him if that was because he felt the money would be safer there or if it was so he could earn money on it in a bank. He said, "The second one!" Then he asked about how much he would earn. Rates were abysmally low then and I was afraid that he might lose his motivation for the account. I explained that he'd probably only get about 1%, which meant that if he had $100 in his account for an entire year, he'd get about $1. "Well," he said, "that's $1 more than I'd get if I didn't put the money in the bank!" This would be a rewarding moment for any parent, but as a parent who is also a financial planner, it bordered on ecstasy.

Your child shouldn't take money out of her savings account frequently. It should be for big items. We use a matching plan with our kids, much like what many employers have in their retirement plans. Everything that the child puts into her savings account, we provide a contribution that's a percentage of what she put in. You can use a percentage that you feel motivates the child without making it ridiculous. Anything over 50% is probably too much. But a contribution of at least 10% is probably going to get your child's attention and make her want to save. As with any situation where another person's money is involved, there is a catch. The child needs the parent's approval to withdraw money from the account. That keeps the account from having too much in-and-out activity. The child knows that she's going to need your permission to spend the money and, because you've established in her mind what you feel are appropriate large purchases, she knows what you might or might not allow her to buy with the money. Your matching contribution, however, makes her more likely to save money, both for unforeseen short-term purchases or emergencies and for purchases that fulfill long-term goals.

Personal Notes

Siblings

"I tell you of all history the most beautiful product is the family tie."
- Zona Gale

My husband and I are both only children. We both grew up around a lot of cousins and neighborhood families, so we weren't total strangers to the ways of sibling rivalry and the reassurance that blood is thicker than water. But I don't know that anyone is completely ready to deal with sibling issues as a parent until he is faced with them.

That being said, I've seen generally positive results from letting siblings have pretty free rein with their reactions to each others' financial decisions. Our kids generally discuss their money pretty openly in family settings, so the reaction of brothers and sisters can be much more effective than the adult feedback. The kids are, after all, closer to being peers than we are. As parents, we have had to step in on occasion as we would in any situation. "You're not allowed to call your sister the stupidest human being alive. Now apologize." But often, a brother saying to his sister that he thinks she's blowing her money on worthless junk makes more impact than if I said the same thing. Besides censuring the kids for harsh reactions to each other, we will have the occasional "It's not your money and it's not your decision" input for the group.

The other enforcement that brothers and sisters can unintentionally give each other is when one of them sets and reaches a goal while the others look on in envy. The envy, of course, doesn't usually kick in until the goal is reached, but the point generally gets across anyway. A child comes home with something she purchased that her siblings don't have. She actually has the right to say, "I don't have to share. It's mine. I paid for it." And we back her up. The other kids know that if they want that item, they have to save for it.

Make sure you keep that last point in mind. A friend of mine told of a blunder that her mom made when she was growing up. She wanted to get her ears pierced and her mom didn't want her to. The mom told my friend that the only way she'd let her have her ears pierced was if the daughter earned the money for it. My friend said the only job she could get at that age was babysitting, so she babysat herself almost to death getting up the money for the ear piercing. (In those days, babysitting only paid about 50¢ an hour and it cost about $20 to get ears pierced.) Her mom was good to her word and took her to have her ears pierced. The process was so simple that the mom was sold on it and took all of the rest of her daughters to get their ears pierced—and the mom paid for it. My friend was furious and her mom didn't understand what her problem was. (Don't worry. This moment of questionable parenting was an aberration and the mom and my friend had a good relationship for the rest of the time they were both alive.)

Which brings up a major point with siblings. It's overly simplistic to say that all the kids need to be treated the same. They aren't all the same. When I look at my three kids, they completely refute all evidence for a common gene pool once you get past physical appearances. They have different interests, priorities, and learning styles. When kids say, "We all need to be treated the same" a good response might be "So if your sister is grounded, should I ground you, too?" Of course the answer is no, but there needs to be equity. Each child needs to have the comparable consequences for similar actions and decisions. There are no easy answers there, but the kids are keeping score of inconsistencies. Count on it. This is especially true when they are close in age. So when you are deciding what is fair, don't make a snap decision. Think through what it will teach to each of your kids, not just the one who has put the issue in front of you.

Personal Notes

_____
_____
_____
_____
_____
_____
_____
_____
_____
_____
_____
_____
_____
_____
_____
_____
_____
_____
_____
_____

Taxes

"Taxes are what we pay for civilized society."
-Oliver Wendell Holmes, Jr.

As adults, taxes are a reality that we learn to live with. There are three basic kinds and kids need to have exposure to at least two of these as they affect them so they can learn to plan for them in their finances. The three major types are income tax, sales tax, and property tax, which is also sometimes called an excise tax. For those who work for a company that pays via a traditional paycheck, the taxes are taken out. We can learn how to have them take more or less than might be our actual tax bill, but it's pretty much a given that we're going to pay taxes. Anyone who is self-employed and didn't plan properly during that first profitable year for the coming tax hit has a fearsome awe of the need to take taxes into account.

There are differing approaches to introducing kids to taxes that have credence. Some people believe that kids need to know that some of their money will go to taxes as soon as they receive their first allowance. One parent shared with me that he pays each of his kids allowance, but they must immediately pay back something to their parents for taxes, room, board, and utilities. So the children in that family believe that taxes have the same weight in financial decisions as basic living expenses. Not a bad lesson.

The other method is learning through a first paycheck. This is the method that I have personally utilized. We financial geeks really get a big laugh out of stories about a young person looking at a first paycheck and saying, "Who is FICA and why is he getting so much of my money?" Learning about taxes is certainly an advantage of earning money from a "real" employer. It really brings home that working for two hours at $8 an hour does not put $16 dollars in your pocket.

In terms of seeing taxes in a positive way, we owe it to our kids as parents to point out what taxes do for us. Your political views may skew whether you stress the advantage of social programs, military, or a balance of both, but the government does provide services that it's difficult for individuals to provide without some type of public infrastructure. There are also local and regional services that are provided through some type of tax. Roads, police and fire protection, museums, parks, cultural services, and food banks are often funded, in whole or in part, from somewhere other than the national government. As your children are grousing about paying tax out of their money, point out what we get from taxes.

Sales tax is easy to forget until you get to the checkout counter. This is a type of tax that a child should get used to as soon as she is purchasing things with her own money. Any community that has a sales tax is a good educational ground for kids realizing they need to pay tax. When a child saves for a purchase, help her calculate in advance how much the tax will be so she'll have enough for that. If she can't pay the tax, she's not really buying the item on her own. Often there are contingencies involved in a purchase anyway, so it's wise to have something more than the exact price of the item when you walk into a store. A friend once told a story about the Girl Scout troop for which she was a leader. As a holiday activity, she took all the girls shopping for gifts for their parents. Each girl brought the amount she could spend and was given half an hour to shop and be ready to check out with her purchase. They all went to the check-out counter and it became immediately obvious that none of the girls had planned for sales tax. The leader told me there's no way she was going to endure the whining and extra time involved in each girl taking back the chosen gift and picking a new one. So she just paid the tax for all the girls. It was a lesson that literally cost her.

Even property tax needs to be touched on with kids. A car is probably the first big exposure to this. Not only does the car need gas, insurance, and regular maintenance, once a year in many states the owner pays a tax for it. This cost is worth investigating before the purchase, because it can vary greatly between vehicles. Your child can include this in the research she does before buying the car.

Personal Notes

Vacations

"Why do people so love to wander?"
- Mary Cassatt

A family vacation can be a terrifying money pit or it can be another opportunity for your children to be responsible for their own financial decisions. If your vacations fall in the money pit category, you're constantly having to decide on the spot if you'll buy what your child is asking for. You might also be dealing with some scenes caused by a road-weary child screaming when you won't get the one thing she's allegedly wanted all her life. A trip budget is a wonderful thing. Give each child a specified amount and make it clear that it's up to each of them to decide what to spend the money on. There are a few factors that can make this a positive part of the vacation for the children.

The first thing to be aware of is establishing a realistic budget. We took a very nice trip to Disney World with our family. We established a budget up front that we thought was reasonable for a 10-day vacation. The first night we got in just in time to go to dinner, and on the way one of our daughters saw a Minnie Mouse doll that she wanted. The price of it was her entire budget. We pointed out that the doll would use her whole budget and that it was only the first day of the trip. She was unmoved. She wanted the doll. We finally managed to convince her to wait a day to make the purchase. That night my husband and I discussed it. We knew when we planned the vacation that it would be more expensive than our average vacation, but we hadn't given the kids an "above average" budget. We agreed on an enhanced budget for the kids and told them about it before they went to bed. Our daughter was able to get the Minnie Mouse (which she enjoyed for a lot of years) in addition to several items that either had long- or short-term enjoyment. On a later vacation we went to Hershey Park, Pennsylvania Amish country, and the beach at Ocean City, Maryland. On this trip, the kids didn't get nearly as large a budget. Unless there is a compelling reason, all siblings should have the same budget. If they are old enough, give them the cash and let them carry it with them. Make sure, though, that they can handle that responsibility. It can ruin your child's vacation as well as yours to have her leave her money somewhere or have it stolen. Decide what constitutes a trip that deserves a budget, too. For a while we could hardly be in the car for an hour without one of the kids asking if they got a budget for the trip. Let's be realistic. What is there to buy at Grandma's house?

With a budget like this, the big question the child eventually brings up is "What if I don't spend it all on the vacation?" The answer needs to be that she gets to keep it. Otherwise, she's going to feel like she has to buy things or she'll lose the money. Good for her if she goes home with money in her pocket. You'll want to praise her for that.

On our Disney World trip, my son didn't spend all of his money. Toward the end of the trip we were resting and he said, "Mom, do you think I've spent my budget wisely?" I replied by listing some of the things he'd purchased: a handheld video game, a misting fan, and some other things that weren't intended to last long, to name a few. I also pointed out that he still had money left. I said that yes, I felt he'd made some very wise purchases, some of which he would enjoy for quite a while and some of which he'd enjoyed for the short time they were supposed to last. But it was just as important how he felt about how wisely he'd used the budget, so how did he feel about it? He said he felt good, but had wanted to know what I thought, too.

Some families choose to tell the kids far enough in advance when a vacation is coming and where they'll be going. Then it's up to the kids to save their own money for the trip. This is also a valid way to manage vacation spending. After all, you don't get an automatic budget from your earnings to spend on vacations. If your child doesn't have much opportunity to earn extra money for a vacation, though, she might not be able to have enough to spend on a vacation. Think it through several months before your next trip and you can decide what works for your family.

In order to discourage desperate spur-of-the-moment purchases, try to allow some time for going back to get things. In other words, if you child wants to buy an item, but you think it might not be what she wants, ask her if she'd like to think about it and tell her you can come back by that vendor later in the day or on another day. Also, since you don't want her making rushed decisions, allow some time in your schedule each day for browsing. Another nice time commitment is to look over what each child has purchased during the day and let them tell you what they like about it. Or just make a comment about how much they've enjoyed it or how good it looks on them. This is a place where siblings can sometimes make a point better than you. If your son blows his budget on the first day on things that are broken a few days into the trip and your daughter saves her money and makes some great purchases, chances are good that she'll point that out to him. You might need to intervene before things get really ugly, but the point still gets across.

Decide up front what is and isn't covered by the budget. It's to be assumed that you pay for hotels, meals, and transportation. Our rule of thumb is that we buy family treats. For instance, if the family stops to cool off with a drink or ice cream, we buy. If we offer everyone a drink and one of the kids wants an ice cream, we'll let her have an ice cream instead of a drink if the prices are comparable. If she wants both, we'll buy the drink and she can either buy the ice cream or do without. We'll do the same thing if we all get a souvenir t-shirt or hat. Also, my husband and I will usually find a spot during the trip where we tell the kids that they can each have a treat from us. It might be that we let them each pick a souvenir from a specific group of comparably price items, or we might tell them each that they can get something up to a specified price in a shop we're in. If they want something outside the amount allotted, they have the option to pay the difference.

You want your vacation to be free of the pressure of feeling like you need to either make buying decisions or refuse to pay for things. Once the vacation is set and you know how much the budget will be, tell the kids. Let them know the budget amount and be clear that they don't get it until you arrive at the trip destination. You can tell them the type of things they may and may not buy and they can ask questions about the parameters prior to the trip. Even if you discuss or even discourage a purchase as they're thinking about it, it'll be much easier on you—and them—than debating your way through each souvenir shop.

Vehicles

> "An adventure is only an inconvenience rightly considered."
> - G.K. Chesterton

A car is probably the biggest purchase for a child prior to actually living on his own. There are several legitimate ways to approach a car purchase.

Many parents feel strongly that a child won't have a car unless he buys it. If that is the approach you'd like to take, you and your child should not assume that this means you have no say in the process. In some states no one can enter into a contract to purchase or borrow unless he is legally an adult, so he'll need your cooperation anyway. Your child should have to research any vehicle he buys before he can purchase it.

- What is its safety rating?
- How well does the car hold its value?

- How many miles to the gallon does it get?
- What would insurance run on the car?

You can insist that the purchase of a vehicle doesn't move forward unless research is done. If your child will own the car, he needs to save up the amount of the insurance deductible as well as the first insurance premium payment and the price of the car or down payment before he is allowed to buy, as well as having a credible explanation of how he will pay his own insurance premium on a regular basis. You need to have a veto on his car of choice if it doesn't meet with your safety requirements.

Once he has the car, maintenance, gas, insurance, and other obligations are his. If you take on any part of that, you have to have a reason other than bailing him out of over- commitment. Feel free to offer observations and suggestions, but it's up to him if he takes them. Safety is the area where you should quickly step in and take over. If he is in an accident or exhibits behaviors that might be dangerous, you can step in and take away some of his autonomy regarding when and how he can drive the car. The worst case scenario if safety is an issue is that you take possession of the car and sell it. The best case is that he makes a wise choice of vehicles, keeps it well maintained, pays for it, and becomes more financially and personally responsible.

Another alternative is to have a car available for your child. You set the parameters for who drives the car when and what are acceptable places and activities that include the car. This may seem like a cop-out on making your child responsible for his own finances. However, there are a couple of reasons this may be a better learning experience. First of all, a vehicle should not be a higher priority than solid academic achievement and non-school activities that will provide growth opportunities for your child. If he gets a job so he can have a car, he might not be able to join an extracurricular club that could lead to a career he'd find rewarding. Also, if your child is involved in enriching activities, he needs to get to them somehow. If you need to take him all the time, that may be a big imposition on you personally and professionally. It also doesn't give him a sense of independence. There is definitely a fine line here. You don't want your child to feel that independence is driving your car, but the sense of responsibility can be established in other ways. For instance, if you pay for the car, maintenance, and gas, make the child responsible for getting the car to the mechanic for oil changes, tire rotation, gas fill-ups, and other things that need to be done. A child who is busy during the school year might have a summer job. You could establish ahead of time that a specific financial commitment will be required when the child has a job. Don't leave that commitment unknown. Either set a dollar amount or a percentage that the child will need to contribute to auto care. Again, there may be a better use of your child's time than a summer job. What if he got an opportunity to travel abroad for the summer and study with a mentor in his chosen field? That sounds much better for his long-term growth than paying for a few oil changes.

Personal Notes

Final Note

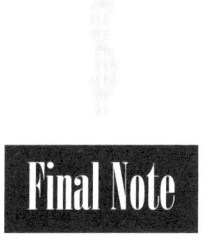

"Trust yourself. You know more than you think you do."
– Benjamin Spock

The concepts here work. The method you use needs to fit your family. While the specific strategies here are tested, they might not be the right ones for you. Start with what feels right for you while offering freedom and responsibility to your kids. If you need to make some adjustments, you can do that and discuss with your kids why the changes are necessary. One nice by-product of this method is it opens the lines of communication. If you and your kids can learn to talk openly about money while they're young, you'll be great resources for each other as they grow into adults.

If you've come up with a teaching example that matches this philosophy that you'd like to share, send it to ideas@brightleitz.com . I plan to do a compilation at a later date. If one of your ideas is used, you'll get a free copy of that book.

Have fun!

THE APPENDIX

A Bright Leitz Money Map Book

Money Smart Kids

Future Goals

Goal_____
Total Cost_____

Date	Amount Added	Total Saved

The Beauty of Smart, Long Term Investing

	Investor A			**Investor B**	
	Invests $3,000 per year 22 thru 30 with 8% compound return			Invests $3,000 per year 31 thru 60 with 8% compound return	
AGE	INVESTED	TOTAL ACCUMULATED	AGE	INVESTED	TOTAL ACCUMULATED
22	$3,000	$3,000	22		
23	$3,000	$6,240	23		
24	$3,000	$9,739	24		
25	$3,000	$13,518	25		
26	$3,000	$17,600	26		
27	$3,000	$22,008	27		
28	$3,000	$26,768	28		
29	$3,000	$31,910	29		
30	$3,000	$37,463	30		
31		$40,460	31	$3,000	$3,000
32		$43,696	32	$3,000	$6,240
33		$47,192	33	$3,000	$9,739
34		$50,968	34	$3,000	$13,518
35		$55,045	35	$3,000	$17,600
36		$59,449	36	$3,000	$22,008
37		$64,204	37	$3,000	$26,768
38		$69,341	38	$3,000	$31,910
39		$74,888	39	$3,000	$37,463
40		$80,879	40	$3,000	$43,460
41		$87,349	41	$3,000	$49,936
42		$94,337	42	$3,000	$56,931
43		$101,884	43	$3,000	$64,486
44		$110,035	44	$3,000	$72,645
45		$118,838	45	$3,000	$81,456
46		$128,345	46	$3,000	$90,973
47		$138,613	47	$3,000	$101,251
48		$149,702	48	$3,000	$112,351
49		$161,678	49	$3,000	$124,339
50		$174,612	50	$3,000	$137,286
51		$188,581	51	$3,000	$151,269
52		$203,667	52	$3,000	$166,370
53		$219,961	53	$3,000	$182,680
54		$237,558	54	$3,000	$200,294
55		$256,562	55	$3,000	$219,318
56		$277,087	56	$3,000	$239,863
57		$299,254	57	$3,000	$262,052
58		$323,194	58	$3,000	$286,016
59		$349,050	59	$3,000	$311,898
60		**$376,974**	60	$3,000	**$339,850**

Investor C

Invests $3,000 per year 22 thru 60
with 8% compound return

AGE	INVESTED	TOTAL ACCUMULATED
22	$3,000	$3,000
23	$3,000	$6,240
24	$3,000	$9,739
25	$3,000	$13,518
26	$3,000	$17,600
27	$3,000	$22,008
28	$3,000	$26,768
29	$3,000	$31,910
30	$3,000	$37,463
31	$3,000	$43,460
32	$3,000	$49,936
33	$3,000	$56,931
34	$3,000	$64,486
35	$3,000	$72,645
36	$3,000	$81,456
37	$3,000	$90,973
38	$3,000	$101,251
39	$3,000	$112,351
40	$3,000	$124,339
41	$3,000	$137,286
42	$3,000	$151,269
43	$3,000	$166,370
44	$3,000	$182,680
45	$3,000	$200,295
46	$3,000	$219,318
47	$3,000	$239,863
48	$3,000	$262,052
49	$3,000	$286,016
50	$3,000	$311,898
51	$3,000	$339,850
52	$3,000	$370,038
53	$3,000	$402,641
54	$3,000	$437,852
55	$3,000	$475,880
56	$3,000	$516,950
57	$3,000	$561,306
58	$3,000	$609,211
59	$3,000	$660,948
60	$3,000	**$716,824**

A Bright Leitz Money Map Book

Money Smart Kids

Living Expenses

	Monthly	Annual	Comments
After Tax Income:			
Husband			
Wife			
Other			
Total			
Expenses:			
Housing Expenses (Mortgage, Rent, Ins)			
Household Expenses (Maint, Furniture)			
Utilities			
Phone/Cable/Garbage			
Meals Outside of Home			
Groceries			
Personal Care			
Child Care			
Clothing			
Vehicles Payments			
Other Vehicle Expenses (Gas, Maint, Ins)			
Life Insurance			
Medical Insurance			
Other Medical/Dental Expenses			
Retirement Plan			
College Funding			
Gifts			
Travel and Entertainment			
Charitable Contributions			
Miscellaneous			
Total			
Income Less Expenses			

Used with permission from Pinnacle Financial Concepts, Inc.

About the Author

Linda Leitz is a Certified Financial Planner™, Enrolled Agent with the IRS, and has been in the financial industry since 1979. She specializes in helping families and individuals with their long term financial goals. Through Pinnacle Financial Concepts, Inc., she assists her clients with Investments, Retirement Planning, Education Funding, Estate Planning, Tax Planning, Goal Setting and Professional Coaching. Linda is also a Certified Divorce Financial Analyst and helps people in the midst of a divorce resolve financial issues through Divorce Solutions, Inc. Linda writes and speaks on family finances.

Before becoming a financial planning professional, Linda held executive positions in the banking industry in management, credit administration, and loan portfolio management. She began her career as a bank examiner. She has a BBA in Business Administration from Principia College and an MBA from Southern Methodist University. She has also had extensive community involvement. Linda and her husband Butch have three children.